Rules & Tools for Leaders

Perry M. Smith

Avery Publishing Group

Garden City Park, New York

Cover Designers: Douglas Brooks
    and William Gonzalez
In-house Editor: Helene Ciaravino
Typesetter: Elaine V. McCaw
    and James Ross
Printer: Paragon Press, Honesdale, PA

Avery Publishing Group
120 Old Broadway
Garden City Park, NY 11040
1–800–548–5757

Library of Congress Cataloging-in-Publication Data

Smith, Perry M.
    Rules & tools for leaders : how to run an organization
    successfully / by Perry M. Smith
        p.   cm.
    Includes bibliographical references and index.
    ISBN 0–89529–835–X
    1. Leadership. 2. Executives 3. Management 4. Organization
    I. Title.
    HD57.7.S69   1998   98–17845
    658.4′092– – dc21   CIP

Printed in the United States of America
10 9 8 7 6

CONTENTS

To Connor, the lovely and talented lady who has shared with me the joys and the heartaches of leadership in so many settings.

ACKNOWLEDGMENTS

Many hundreds of people assisted me in the preparation of this book. First and foremost, I must thank the students of the National War College, the students of the Industrial College of the Armed Forces, and some international students from the National Defense University, who took my courses on executive leadership. These mature public servants from five military services, a dozen civilian agencies, and ten foreign nations critiqued this book in manuscript form and helped me to develop my ideas, as well as to clarify and polish my rules of thumb, checklists, and case studies.

Second, I must acknowledge the substantive contributions of my guest speakers who took the time to share their experiences as they ran some of the largest organizations in this country: John Gardner; Verne Orr; Ambassador Bill Harrop; Walt Ulmer; Bob Springer; Bill Maloney; Tom Pownall; Bob Kirk; and Vice Admiral James Stockdale.

Special thanks are due to Mary McNabb and Yvette Taylor, who took dictation by the hour and typed the initial manuscript; Patricia Pasquarett, who carried out many typing and editing duties; Cathy Salvato, who accomplished many editorial chores; Sherwood (Woody) Goldberg, who helped restructure the manuscript at a critical phase; and to Fred Kiley, Don Anderson, Walter "R" Thomas, Laura Conk, Jack Jacobs, Mike Miller, Charlie and Jane Hamm, Bob and Harriet Plowden, Ed Parks, Bill Clover, Jim Simms, Bob Sorley, Buddy Diamond, and Ken Wenker, for their valuable input and editorial comments.

A wonderful group of people gave me assistance when I decided to publish the revised edition. John Barry; Norty Schwartz; Dick Chilcoat; Frank Brady; Bob Murphy; Jim

Blackwell; Joe Leboeuf; Dierdre Dixon; Lissa Young; David Haughey; John Fryer; Scott and Stacie Morgan; Doc Bahnsen; Fred Warren; David Kozak, Bob Elder, and Robert Fant. Each one of these people, despite their busy schedules, spent many hours carefully reviewing the book in an effort to make the new version much better than the first. David Haughey deserves special thanks for reading the text three times and then sending in his comments from each reading.

Thanks are also due to Rudy Shur, Diana Puglisi, and Helene Ciaravino of Avery Publishing Group. Their helpful suggestions and careful attention to detail were greatly appreciated.

And last but not least, my thanks go to Connor Smith, who critiqued and edited the manuscript and put up with a husband who, once again, was inspired to write and rewrite.

FOREWORD

Running a large organization is challenging work. It also can be rewarding and uplifting. Good management, characterized by sound leadership, judgment, and integrity, is required in virtually any endeavor. Although there are many good books on management and leadership, what has been needed is a short, down-to-earth guide for busy leaders, to help them cope with the tougher issues. Perry Smith has written that guide, and leaders and associates alike can benefit from his ideas, insights, and rules of thumb.

What is most refreshing about *Rules & Tools for Leaders* is the clarity of language and the crispness of the author's writing style. He gets to his points fast. This is a "tuned in" book. It deals with the real issues, legitimate dilemmas, and myriad possibilities that confront leaders. With extensive experience in running organizations, along with teaching and research in leadership and management, Smith has accomplished what many others would love to have done; he has written a guide that both leaders and associates can use to be more effective in their professional lives.

There is a deceptive simplicity to this sophisticated volume. In one sense, it is the thoughtful reader's "how-to" book in the field of management. Those of us who have tried to learn plumbing or golf in this manner know that it can have its limitations. It is unrealistic to believe that anyone will become master of all he or she surveys in an executive suite as the result of one quick pass through *Rules & Tools for Leaders*. On the other hand, you have come to the right place if you are interested in a working visit with a talented, knowledgeable, and highly articulate executive who has many valuable perceptions to share.

Most importantly, I believe Perry Smith's ideas are likely to get your own creative juices flowing wherever you reside, or want to reside, in your particular organizational environment. This is the kind of book that many readers will want to keep in their libraries and periodically revisit for various aspects of its diverse contents.

Actually, some of Smith's ideas invite a double take the first time around. For example, there is the "no nonconcurrence through silence rule," a wonderful way to keep the lines of communication open between a leader and his or her staff. Then there is the "'oh, by the way' problem," alluding to the managerial hazard of snap decisions. In contrast, the "60-percent decision rule" shows the way to managers who tilt toward timidity more often than impetuosity in the decision-making process.

Beyond the case studies and checklists, and the chapters ranging from strategic planning to personal introspection, *Rules & Tools for Leaders* has a deeper and wider application. We live in an era of unprecedented commercial, technological, and military challenge. We earn our daily bread in an increasingly competitive environment; markets have taken on truly global proportions. How well our nation manages its considerable assets—how effectively our government, industry, and other institutions utilize human, material, and financial resources—obviously is a critical factor in determining the prosperity of the future. It is as simple, and as complex, as that. Fortunately, management and leadership skills can be strengthened through learning. *Rules & Tools for Leaders* contributes to developing, honing, and refining these essential skills in a very specific way. The beneficiaries will be not only individual leaders and their organizations, but, ultimately, the confederation that we call the free enterprise system.

For further information, as the old saying goes, inquire within.

—Norman R. Augustine
Former Chairman and Chief Executive Officer
Lockheed Martin Corporation

PREFACE

For many years, I looked for a practical guide to running organizations. Since such a guidebook was nowhere to be found, I decided to write one myself. I did so while serving as the Commandant of, and teaching courses on executive development and on leadership at, the National War College in Washington, DC—the senior professional school for career civilian and military officials with the highest potential for leadership.

Rules & Tools for Leaders should not be considered scholarly treatise, for it breaks no new conceptual ground on leadership or management. I designed it for those busy leaders who might have a few hours on an airplane or on a quiet Sunday afternoon. This short book contains hundreds of helpful hints on dealing with the tough issues that lie ahead. The text is also designed for associates who must deal with their bosses and are interested in understanding the problems and dilemmas that these leaders might be facing. In addition, it is structured suitably for use in management and leadership courses, to augment the more theoretical works that are available in the literature.

I have had the great pleasure of having been in charge of a number of organizations, as well as a few staff directorates. *I have written the book that I would liked to have had when I was in leadership positions.* This book offers many rules of thumb, checklists, and case studies to spark the interest of the reader. *Rules & Tools for Leaders* is a very personal book; it attempts to incorporate the numerous insights that I gained over more than thirty years of work in organizations in the United States and in five other nations.

In the last three years of my military career, I had the luxury that few leaders enjoy—the luxury of time: time for reflection; time for teaching; time for research; and time for writing. Teaching a leadership course for three consecutive years to some of the best and brightest people provided extraordinary insights. In those three years, I taught five seminars. My 136 students came from all of the military services of the United States, from many civilian agencies of the Federal Government, and from such nations as Israel, Egypt, the Philippines, Korea, Peru, Great Britain, the Federal Republic of Germany, Jordan, Pakistan, India, and the Somali Republic. (Of the international students, one had led an Israeli Army Division into combat in Lebanon; another had been the mayor of a city of 500,000 inhabitants in the Philippines; and a third had led a Sikh brigade into the Punjab to root out Sikh terrorists). Most had already run small or medium-sized organizations, but all wanted to learn more and share their ideas. Each student wrote papers, participated actively in the seminar environment, challenged my views, and forced me to revisit, in greater depth, my own experiences as a leader. To have been the Commandant of the National War College, which is a great historical national institution, and to have had the privilege of teaching such distinguished public servants was a deeply rewarding and uplifting experience. Many of the perceptions in this book came from this group.

Since 1986, I have spent most of my time teaching leadership, mostly in the corporate world. It has been an incredibly broadening experience for me. The more I teach, the more I learn. For example, conducting a leadership workshop for twenty-five Microsoft executives is wonderfully challenging and rewarding. Tossing out leadership ideas to smart people who haven't had much leadership education but are eager to learn is almost as much fun as flying the F-15 fighter aircraft. Bringing leadership ideas from the military to corporate executives continues to be a great joy. In turn, bringing the best of the leadership techniques developed by such visionary companies as E Systems, UPS, Texas Instruments, Lockheed Martin, and Microsoft to government agencies and military war and staff colleges is equally uplifting.

Finally, I had the privilege of interviewing a number of

chief executive officers and presidents of various corporations, banks, schools and universities, and think tanks, to gain their insights into leadership outside the governmental context. These busy leaders had read an earlier version of this book and, as a result, were able to give me some very specific input on the points that I had raised, the guidelines, the checklists, and the case studies. I have listed none of these individuals since I have used a number of their experiences, some of which touch on delicate issues. Of course, I thank them all.

Leaders count. People at the top can—should—make a difference. Leaders decide whether you can vote, what music you will hear, which neighborhoods will be wiped out by a new highway, and whether you will have to give a blood sample to get or keep a job. By setting standards, by establishing and maintaining a network of communications, by nurturing relationships, and by motivating associates, a leader molds the daily performance of an organization. Furthermore, a leader permanently can affect an organization by creating and implementing a strategic vision with specific long-term goals. The future is not determined already. What will happen in the next twenty or thirty years will be, in large part, the consequence of decisions that influential leaders make within their organizations today. *Rules & Tools for Leaders* advises you on how to make those decisions in an organized, intelligent, and insightful manner.

—Perry M. Smith
Augusta, Georgia

INTRODUCTION

This is a very basic book to help managers, supervisors, and administrators to be better leaders. If you are looking for concepts, philosophies, paradigms, or academic treatises, this definitely is not the book for you. Put it back on the shelf now. But if you are looking for a handy, up-to-date tool kit and guidebook on leadership, you have come to the right place. This book will serve as a source of advice as you develop your leadership skills, and as a double check when you are making a tough decision for your organization.

Rules & Tools for Leaders is designed to allow executives to dive easily into the pages at a time of need. You are about to hire someone? Go to my hiring checklist. You need to fire someone? Reread the short chapter on firing and glance at the firing checklist. You are frustrated by your meetings? Use the meeting checklist. You are about to take over a big job? The transition chapter will be helpful.

This is a book written by someone who has been in charge of a number of organizations. I personally have experienced both failure and achievement as a leader, and have taken careful notes along the way. The setbacks provided the most valuable lessons, but I also gained knowledge and insight from some successful ventures. My approach stems not only from my extensive military experience at West Point, out in the field, in combat, and at the Pentagon, but also from my work with several major organizations, including CNN, Duke Power, Tiffany and Company, Caterpillar, The Kellogg Foundation, and Microsoft.

I have boiled down the very best of what I have learned about leadership and put it into *Rules & Tools for Leaders*. People who have read earlier versions of this book often comment to me that what they like most is the straightforward language and the handy checklists. In fact, in autographing copies that people have owned for some time, I often notice that pages are dog-eared—a wonderful indication that the book has been used quite often. It is designed not simply to be *read* once, but to be *used* time and time again.

    Rules & Tools for Leaders is your checklist for the future. Use it well, and use it often. Pass it around to your colleagues. Let me know how I can improve it. Write to me at PO Box 15666, Augusta, Georgia 30919, or telephone: (706) 738–9133; e-mail: gencnn@aol.com; web site: http://members.aol.com/gencnn.

    Good reading and good leading.

1
LEADING
thirty fundamentals to remember

A leader is a man who has the ability to get other people to do what they don't want to do, and like it.
> —Harry S. Truman

Leadership and learning are indispensable to each other.
> —John F. Kennedy

There are thirty key fundamentals that form the basis for my approach to leadership. While many of these fundamentals will be discussed in greater detail later in this book, they are presented here to help the reader understand the foundations of my thinking on the art of leadership.

1. Trusting

It is essential that the leaders of large organizations be able to trust subordinate leaders and other associates. This is a difficult task for those who want to direct every aspect of their organizations. Such leaders cannot find their way clear to trust people and, as a result, they do not nurture subleaders or give them the opportunity to exercise their full creative talents. Being a truly effective leader requires a great deal of trust in associates, balanced with a willingness to remove people who cannot be trusted—a facet of leadership that necessitates tough decision-making. Without trust and other elements of mutual respect among leaders and their associates, an organization often will suffer a combination of low performance and poor morale. In the words of Frank Crane, "You may be deceived if you trust too much, but you will live in torment if you do not trust enough."

2.   *Teaching*

Teachership and leadership go hand-in-glove. Leaders must be willing to teach skills, to share insights and experiences, and to work very closely with people to help them mature and be creative. In order to be good teachers, leaders must be well-organized individuals, good communicators, and goal-setters. By teaching, leaders can inspire, motivate, and influence associates at all levels. (See Chapter 13.)

3.   *Communicating Creatively*

If a leader is a good writer, communication, both up and down the organizational structure, will occur in a way that is meaningful, understandable, and has impact. If a good editor, the leader can work on papers, issues, and problems that come in written form, to ensure that the final product is clear and produces the maximum positive impact. If a good speaker, the leader can "reach out," making people feel good about themselves and encouraging them to take pride in their work. Creative communication is fundamental to effective leadership.

4.   *Squinting with the Ears*

Listening is the most important skill for leaders. Introverts have a great edge, since they tend to listen quietly and usually aren't "interruptaholics." Too many extroverts are thinking about what they will say next, rather than hearing what is being said now. This is called "fake listening." Whereas introverts are natural listeners, extroverts need help in gaining and maintaining this essential skill. All extroverts should read and heed *Effective Listening*, a short book by Kevin Murphy. If a leader is a good listener, he or she can accept ideas, criticism, and other feedback that can improve the organization and create an atmosphere of excellence and caring. In the words of an unknown sage, "I never learned anything while I was talking."

5.   *Avoiding the Role of Chief Problem Solver*

Leaders should facilitate problem solving, but should let associates solve most problems. The psychic reward—the sense of achievement—that someone gets from actually solving a problem is quite important. It builds self-esteem and enhances the associate's ability to do still better in subsequent situations. Even though leaders often can solve the problems more quickly than others, it is poor practice to be the problem solver. There are, of course, occasional exceptions to this rule. At times when the organization is in serious trouble, when associates appear unable to formulate a good answer to a problem, or when only the leader has the expertise, the understanding, or the contacts to make the right decisions, the leader should step in. By being problem solvers of last resort, leaders can help their organizations to grow and thrive. General George Patton advised, "Never tell people how to do things. Tell them what needs doing and they will surprise you with their ingenuity."

6. Building Stamina

The demands of leadership are very heavy and no matter how well executives may plan their daily, weekly, and monthly schedules, there will be times when the pressures and demands will be onerous. Even though leaders may be very tired, they must be able to reach within themselves to find the reservoir of energy and creativity to handle crisis situations and other tough decisions. An intellectual and physical fitness program is essential for executives who wish to be prepared for these difficult periods. Fundamentally, if leaders cannot take care of themselves, how can they create climates that provide care for others?

7. Managing and Using Time Effectively

One of the great faults of American executives is their general failure to discipline their schedules, their "in-boxes," their telephones, their travel commitments, and their meetings. Unlike many of their European and East Asian counterparts, American executives are often caught up in "activity traps" that fill up their days, keep them very busy, and allow little time for thoughtful reflection and strategic thinking. Staying busy and working very long hours are not necessarily measurements of leadership effectiveness. Leaders should control their schedules, at least in part, and there are many techniques and skills that can help them do so. (See Chapter 8.)

8.   *Maintaining Technical Competence*

Executives must understand their businesses so that, as they carry out day-to-day activities, they know what they are doing. It is necessary that leaders not only understand the major elements of the organizations that they head, but also that they keep up with the changes. Otherwise, they do not grasp exactly what their daily activities produce. Furthermore, if a leader has a high level of technical competence, then he or she should be able to trust intuition. This combination of competence and intuition can be extremely powerful. Leaders probably would not have reached their present positions without good intuition; they should continue to trust it. They should ask themselves if they are satisfied with their own decisions, if their associates' decisions are acceptable, or if something seems wrong. To quote Ralph Waldo Emerson, "The essence of genius is spontaneity and instinct. Trust thyself." Part of intuition is having "antennae" out, keeping a hand on the pulse of the organization, and being "street-smart" and "in touch." In other words, effective leaders take a second look when things seem suspicious.

9.   *Dealing with Incompetence*

Leaders must be willing to set standards, to abide by those standards unwaveringly, and to require their associates to live by those standards. They are responsible for ensuring that missions are accomplished. Inhibitors to this task, such as the continued presence of ineffective associates, drain the organization and its capable leaders of the time, energy, and attention needed to accomplish the set goals. In such circumstances, leaders have a responsibility to remove those who stand in the way of success. Almost everyone within a given organization knows who is competent and who is not. The leader's actions (or non-actions) in dealing with incompetent people are seen by all. By allowing incompetent associates to stay in positions of responsibility, leaders are not serving themselves, the institutions, and, in many cases, the incompetent employees well. When it is necessary to remove people from key positions, leaders should meet personally with those individuals. Removals should be done with grace and style, but also with firmness. (See Chapter 21.)

10.   Taking Care of People

Leaders should recognize not just the top performers, but also the many others who are competently doing their jobs with good attitudes and a strong commitment to institutional goals. Making continuous efforts—during the morning, at noontime, and before leaving in the evening—to thank people is an important part of taking care of them. Acts of gratitude contribute to their psychological health. Furthermore, leaders should mentor outstanding associates, while avoiding the pitfalls of cronyism. When it comes to appreciation and recognition, Pierce Chapron offers helpful advice: "He who receives a benefit should never forget it; he who bestows should never remember it." (See Chapter 5 and Chapter 10.)

11.   Providing Vision

Leaders who are not planners are simply caretakers, gatekeepers, and time-servers. Though they may run efficient and effective organizations, leaders do not really serve the long-term interests of their institutions unless they plan, set goals, and provide strategic vision. Leaders who care about their missions and about their people normally desire to leave their organizations in better shape and with a clearer strategic direction than when they took over. Good planning, goal-setting, and priority-setting can accomplish these things and create a marvelous legacy. Leaders who are not visionaries, and many are not, should ensure that they have frequent contact with people who have a talent and an inclination for long-range planning, farsighted thinking, and innovation. By allowing visionaries to be heard, leaders can validate the process of creative, "out-of-the-box" thinking. The most effective leaders are agents for change, and one of the best ways to ensure this change is through good strategic planning. (See Chapter 14.)

12.   Controlling Ambitions and Egos

Often leaders have to subvert their strong personal ambitions in order to make sure that the movements toward higher standards of excellence and performance are accomplished in careful and systematic ways. Selfless, strong leaders gain the respect of associates and the support of superiors. They are willing to say, "I was wrong."; "I made a mistake."; "I accept responsibility for our failure and am willing to accept the *full* consequences of that failure." If leaders are too ambitious for the organization, or too ambitious for themselves, they may drive the organization in dysfunctional directions. In fact, they may become part of the problem rather than part of the solution.

13.   *Planning and Conducting Meetings*

Leaders spend much of their time in meetings. They should establish the ground rules and be actively involved in the meetings, to make sure that they stay on track. Individuals should be given ample opportunity to express their views and their disagreements. Scheduled meetings should have announced start and stop times, so that everyone can plan the rest of the day; for instance, "The 11 a.m. sales meeting will end at noon." It is important to know how to wrap up meetings, to draw conclusions, to set up the time and agenda for the next meeting, and to direct individuals to carry out certain tasks that have resulted from new decisions. A wonderful way to conclude a meeting is for the leader to repeat what he or she has heard and to ask if any major points have been missed (or misunderstood) in the summary. Also, leaders must discontinue regular (weekly, monthly, quarterly) meetings that are not serving an important purpose. American leaders especially must fight the cultural tendency to hold long, undisciplined meetings that yield little useful output.

14.   *Motivating*

Leaders must not only know how to motivate in general, but they should also teach their subordinate leaders so that they, in turn, will be strong in motivational skills. Leaders of larger organizations cannot reach all of their people on a regular basis, so they must count on subordinate leaders to provide much of the motivation. Commitment to mission, love of the job and the people, dedication to high standards, having fun, frequent reinforcement of the organization's plans and goals, strong incentive and reward programs, and lots of compliments for hard work and high performance are all parts of the vital motivation factor.

15. *Being Visible and Approachable*

In large organizations, the four-hour rule is a useful guide: leaders should spend no more than four hours a day in their offices. During the rest of the time, they should be out with their people, conducting meetings, and visiting subordinates in their work areas. Good leaders talk to lower-level officials and get feedback on problem areas. They pat people on the back, make brief and upbeat speeches, hand out awards, and travel widely throughout their establishment or business. In addition, effective leaders make contact with sister organizations, as well as with organizations at higher levels, so they can ensure that important relationships are enhanced and that problem areas are identified as early as possible. (See Chapter 9.)

When they are having meetings or discussions in their offices, leaders should never sit behind their desks. Instead, they should go to a couch or a sofa, thus avoiding an imposing position that is often intimidating to associates. Visitors are more comfortable, and therefore more candid, when leaders sit in the more sociable areas of their offices. The visitors should feel that nothing is more important than the subject that they have come to discuss.

Another aspect of being approachable is getting involved in sports, hobbies, small theater groups, local gatherings, religious activities, etc. In this way, leaders can socialize with associates, having contact with them at various levels. For instance, if a leader jogs with associates, he or she may discover all kinds of interesting things that are occurring in the organization. A lower-level subordinate usually will be more frank on a jogging trail than in an office. Company or unit softball leagues, basketball programs, golf and tennis matches, and volleyball competitions serve the same purpose of enhancing communication and feedback.

Leaders do not have to be athletes. A willingness to take part is all that is needed. The point is to be benignly visible— that is, approachably visible. Some people are often available, but are not approachable. There is one important caution in this regard: a "just-one-of-the-folks" kind of person is normally not a good leader. A leader must be special while still being approachable.

16.   *Using Humor Well*

Most of the time, leaders should laugh at themselves rather than at others. They generally should be willing to tell jokes or even embarrassing stories about their own mistakes, in order to let others know that they are human, that they err, and that they are willing to admit it. Good leaders demonstrate that life is not so important that you can't sit back occasionally and be amused by what's happening. Humor can be a great reliever of tension; a story or a joke at times of crisis or difficulty can be very thera- peutic. Therefore, being relaxed and humorous with people, but not using humor against people, creates a positive atmosphere. Humor that is delivered with an acid tongue and aimed at asso- ciates, however, can be very counterproductive. Off-color humor should be avoided since it diminishes the dignity of leaders and organizations. In addition, leaders should avoid treating *every- thing* as an occasion for humor. Non-stop comedians are unlike- ly to get the respect they need to be effective executives.

17.   *Being Decisive*

Leaders must be decisive—patiently decisive—and not jump as soon as the first individual makes a recommendation for a decision. They should listen to all sides before deciding. In fact, on occasion, it is good practice for a leader to postpone an important decision for a day or two, or even a week or two, while collecting additional information. Leaders should always look for contrasting views and, if at all possible, sleep on important issues. They should talk to their executive offi- cers, deputies, spouses, or other people who can be trusted to forgo personal or parochial interests. In addition, leaders also should talk to people who may not agree with the tentative decisions, to find out what their opposing views might be. However, postponing decisions for many weeks or months is rarely the answer. A non-decision is itself a decision and should be recognized for what it is. Risk-taking is frequently an essential and healthy aspect of decision-making. (See Chapter 7.)

Also, leaders must understand how to implement decisions. If not put into effect, decisions are of little value. So, leaders should know how to develop implementing strategies. Furthermore, they must have follow-up systems to ensure that decisions are not only carried out, but carried out faithfully in both substance and spirit.

18. Observing Themselves

Each person is really five people: you are who you are; you are who you think you are; you are who your subordinate associates think you are; you are who your peers think you are; and you are who your boss thinks you are. Leaders who work hard to get feedback from many sources are more likely to understand and control their various selves and, hence, be better leaders. They should be able to look at themselves objectively and analyze where they have made mistakes, where they have turned people off, and where they have headed down the wrong path. Leaders must be able to look in the mirror and determine what they did right today, what they did wrong today, to which decisions they need to return, and how approachable they were. They should ask themselves if they have been too narrow, too rigid. A trusted confidant can be very helpful in this continuous process of introspection. (See Chapter 16.)

19. Practicing Reliability

A leader should be careful about what commitments are made and, once those commitments are firm, nothing short of major health problems or a very serious crisis in business, institution, or family matters should alter them. Reliability is something that leaders must possess in order to provide stability and strength to their organizations. Important aspects of reliability are persistence and consistency. Leaders should be reasonably flexible, but steadfastness and coherence are important elements of large organizations and deserve the support of leaders at all levels.

20. *Maintaining Open-Mindedness*

The best leaders are the ones whose minds are never closed, who are interested in hearing fresh points of view, and who are eager to deal with new issues. Even after a decision has been made, leaders should be willing to listen to contrary opinions and novel approaches. Although strong leaders do not change their minds too frequently after a major decision has been made, they are not afraid to reconsider, where necessary. Those who *never* reconsider show a degree of rigidity and inflexibility that often spells trouble for the organization.

21. *Maintaining High Standards of Dignity*

When standards of dignity are established and emphasized, everyone can take pride in both the accomplishments and the style of the operation. The leader's role is multifaceted. By dressing well, being well-mannered, avoiding profanity, helping associates through personal or family crises, conducting ceremonies with dignity, welcoming newcomers with warmly written personal letters, etc., leaders can accomplish a great deal. A happy combination of substance and style leads to superb performance and high morale.

22. *Giving Power Away and Making It Stick*

In recent years, there has been much discussion about how to make organizations "empowering" ones. However, empowerment does not necessarily come easy. There are three basic problem areas. Some bosses think leadership is synonymous with control, and refuse to give up any power. A second group of bosses sincerely tries to give power to capable subordinate leaders, but they do not accept it. In such cases, the associates keep giving the power back by checking with the boss, rather than taking action on their own. A third group of bosses gives power away, but quickly grabs it back by micromanaging. Often without realizing it, these bosses ask too many detailed questions and check up on their associates too frequently. Leaders who truly share their power can accomplish extraordinary things. The best leaders understand that leadership is the liberation of talent; hence, they gain power not only by constantly giving it away, but also by not grabbing it back. Making empowerment stick requires much candid discussion, trust, and interaction between leaders and subordinate associates. If real, sustained empowerment is to work well, both leaders and their associates need to "walk their talk" on empowerment and hold up their end of the bargain. (See Chapter 6.)

23. Being Generous and Magnanimous

The golden rule, "Do unto others as you would have them do unto you," is marvelous. However, in leadership situations, the platinum rule may be even better: "Treat others the way they would like to be treated." One of the great joys of leadership is serving associates. Yet leaders often forget to practice servant leadership amidst too many commitments and too large an in-box. If a leader does not help at least five people every day, he or she probably is missing opportunities to uplift himself or herself, as well as the organization. Generosity of time and talent is essential for effective leadership. So is magnanimity, which involves the practice of forgiveness. Some leaders have a terrible time forgiving associates who have fouled things up. Good leaders are willing to pardon those who make honest mistakes. They also pardon themselves when they make errors.

24. Nurturing the Leadership-Followership Relationship

Leadership is not synonymous with authority. It is, to a very considerable extent, a value that is entrusted to superiors by the associates or subordinate leaders. It embodies an emotional, often spiritual investment—a gift of trust. To a great extent, the associates define the conditions under which trust is given. They prescribe the qualities, characteristics, and values that the superior must possess in order to be fully accepted as the leader. It is a wise leader, indeed, who understands and nurtures this relationship between leader and followers, especially with the followers who may not be very visible. These are the fine people, doing great work, who seldom get thanked because they are "invisible." Such associates work so quietly and so competently that they often are not noticed. Without recognition and reward for their outstanding work, their morale will suffer over time. Conversely, leaders should beware of those who try to get a great deal of "face time" with the boss. These folks are often primarily concerned with serving their ambitions or their egos. (See Chapter 10.)

25.   *Welcoming Criticism and Fighting Paranoia*

It is the mature leader, indeed, who accepts even unfair criticism with equanimity, calmness, and grace. Criticism can provide the very useful "reality checks" that all leaders need in order to maintain perspective. Leaders should not want or expect their workers to always agree with the bosses' views and decisions. Therefore, good leaders help associates understand that it is okay to have "love quarrels" with superiors and with the organization. Associates who disagree with the leader are not the enemy. Loyalty and criticism are mutually supportive, while slavish loyalty is deadly. If an associate does something that is terribly painful to the leader, the leader should not assume that it was a deliberate act of maliciousness. A defensive crouch is not a productive response. Wise leaders never attribute to malice that which is adequately explained by stupidity.

Leaders must be brutally honest with themselves or they will slip into the terrible habit of self-deception. Even the best leaders make mistakes. By listening to criticism and quickly catching, acknowledging, and correcting mistakes, good leaders can become superb leaders. (See Chapter 22.)

26.   *Maintaining a Sense of Outrage*

There are too many clever managers who work very hard to keep the boss happy and to stay out of trouble. As a result, they never allow themselves to be outraged when the system is doing serious damage to those who work for them. Instead of deflecting the heat and pressure that is flowing down from above, many managers dump all of it onto their associates. It is much better if leaders take on the issues that are causing grave morale problems. They may not be able to solve the situations promptly, but if they turn away, many people will notice. It is far better to take quick action than to let the situation deteriorate.

Watching bad circumstances eat away at the fabric of an organization because the leader is unwilling to get involved can be terribly depressing.

A specific activity that should stimulate outrage on the part of the leader is when someone tries to practice intimidation. Some managers allow themselves to be intimidated by their own bosses or by outsiders, and, on occasion, even by their subordinate associates. An intimidated boss can never be a great leader. The best leaders and subordinate leaders get mad on occasion and, using controlled outrage, correct the wrongs that are being levied on their people.

27. Learning from Failure

Learning from failure and bouncing back are signposts of good leadership. Bill Gates has an approach to failure that helps explain the great success of Microsoft. He *encourages* failure. In fact, he feels that if Microsoft is not failing on occasion, it must not be pushing hard enough at the boundaries of innovation. Too many leaders take a "zero defects" approach, discourage risk-taking, and punish those who fail. The result is often a slow "death spiral" as the organization misses out on wonderful opportunities, loses its best people, and slides downhill into mediocrity, irrelevance, or bankruptcy. (See Chapter 22.)

28. Building a Robust Braintrust

One of the great success secrets of the best leaders is the building and nurturing of a braintrust. Leaders should be in close contact with two to three hundred brilliant and quick-thinking people outside of their immediate organizations. The members of a braintrust provide great wisdom and experience. Some are experts on important issues. Some are retired and often have the time to do research if they don't have the answers at their fingertips. With an active braintrust, leaders who get stuck and cannot get proper help from their immediate colleagues can find help simply by making a phone call or reaching out over e-mail. Braintrusts offer reciprocal aid; those who participate both receive assistance and give assistance. Within my large braintrust, I have a smaller group who serve as my ethical braintrust.

About once a year, I am confronted with an ethical dilemma and find myself unable to sleep at night. The next morning, I pick up the phone and ask for help. (See Chapter 9.)

29. *Seeking and Cherishing Diversity*

Diversity comes in many packages, and wise leaders seek out and nourish every aspect of it. All organizations should maximize the rich diversity of opinions, heritage, cultures, races, genders, religions, personality types, and attitudes in the American culture. In fact, one of America's greatest strengths is its historic willingness to accept people of different backgrounds. However, too many leaders have a very narrow view of diversity when it comes to hiring new people. They tend to clone themselves and consider diversity only as an afterthought. The best leaders explain to their colleagues, associates, and, most importantly, to their human resources and personnel officials that they want to stress diversity in the hiring process.

30. *Exuding Integrity*

Leaders should not only talk about integrity, but should operate at high levels of integrity. Furthermore, they should emphasize both personal and institutional integrity. Effective leaders take prompt corrective action when there are violations of integrity, and upgrade the standards of institutional integrity over time. They also ensure that everybody understands their fundamental commitment to the values of the organization. Soon after assuming their leadership positions, leaders should look for ways to demonstrate such commitment. Institutional integrity cannot lie dormant until a crisis occurs; it must be ingrained and supported by leaders at all levels. *Of all the qualities that a leader must have, integrity is the most important.* (See Chapter 3.)

2
TAKING OVER
the vital nature of the transition

When ever you are asked if you can do a job, tell em, 'Certainly I can!' Then get busy and find out how to do it.
                                        —*Theodore Roosevelt*

Well begun is half done.
        —*Horace*

Many individuals taking over leadership positions do not think through the transition process. They fail to develop a "take charge" plan, and so they fail to maximize the opportunities to be well-prepared for their new responsibilities. By systematically approaching the transition process and carefully following a checklist, a leader can be much more effective in those critical first few weeks in a new position. The transition process is particularly important for someone coming into a large or complex organization. An executive about to assume the role of leader must deal with the problem of psychological transition, especially if he or she has never run an organization before. This book will help you become a "big" leader by helping you think through the transition to the leadership challenge ahead.

One of the first things that you should do is to ask the present leader to make an audiotape or videotape that addresses major issues, concerns, problems, and frustrations which have occurred in the organization. On this tape, the departing leader should discuss the personalities within the organization, especially those of immediate associates. A frank evaluation of the major personnel problems and a candid analysis of people who need counselling and people who probably should be reas-

17

signed, are invaluable. Additionally, the incumbent should outline any "skeletons in the closet" that exist in the organization,
so that you can be sensitive to issues and problems that might
not be visible during the crucial first few months. Here, a caution is in order: do not accept the information on the tape uncrit-
ically. When listening to the tape, it is important to evaluate the
credibility and impartiality of the previous leader.

Some new leaders prefer not to receive the departing leaders' evaluations of the various strengths and weaknesses of
associates. In such cases, the incoming executive usually desires
to allow the associates a clean slate. I strongly disagree with this
approach. If you play the leadership game with a partial deck of
cards, you can make major mistakes that could do great harm to
the organization. Knowledge of the strengths and weaknesses of
key personnel should be as complete as possible.

If feasible, you should be permitted to have a few weeks to
ask a number of transition questions before assuming new
responsibilities. These queries should be answered (preferably in
writing, but if not, orally) by the present leader, by the deputy, or
by key individuals within the organization. The most important
questions to ask are: "What is the mission, role, or desired output
of the organization?"; "What is the strategic plan?"; "What is the
financial situation?"; "What goals have been established?"; "What
are the priorities?"; "What is the current morale?" Here it would
be advisable to review the organization's most recent evaluations—internal and external reports—to see what steps have
been taken to correct deficiencies. There are a variety of other
questions which a new leader should ask before taking over the
job. Many of these are outlined in Checklist #1 in Appendix A,
and some are discussed below.

*What are the various available means of communication that I can use
to interact creatively with my associates?* Many large organizations
publish newspapers or newsletters on a regular basis. These
publications give you the opportunity to write a column on a
subject that you want to share with your people. Also, local
radio and television are marvelous avenues through which you
can reach out to the members of your team and their families.

Corporate videotapes, e-mail, staff meetings, trips to subordinate organizations, and speeches to various groups are a few more ways in which the active leader can communicate effectively with associates.

Who will report directly to me and how large is my span of control? The careful reading of personnel records ahead of time, as well as discussions with your predecessor and your superior, will help you assess the qualifications of your coworkers and the scope of your duties. A well-connected personnel or human resources director is another important source of information.

What constituencies will I be serving, either directly or indirectly? Leaders normally have to serve many constituencies, including the associates and their families, the customers, the retired community, interest groups, alumni, etc. It is useful to learn who best represents the interests of these constituencies and with whom to meet. As you assume a leadership position, you are automatically assigned an essential role within a communication network. It is essential that you understand that network—both its formal and informal components.

Who is my immediate boss and what are his or her leadership and management styles? Before taking charge, you should meet with your boss and get an explanation of your new job, as well as an understanding of your superior's satisfactions and dissatisfactions with the organization. If your boss feels the organization is in bad shape, you may wish to attempt to reach an understanding about how long it should take to get it back into order. This discussion can lead to some very useful insights concerning both the organization and your boss, including his or her understanding of the problems of organizational rejuvenation. You should also meet with the key staff directors who work for your boss, in order to get their views of the strengths and problem areas within your new organization.

Am I responsible for geographically separated organizations? Do they report directly or indirectly to me? Most large organizations have geographically separated plants, divisions, bureaus, or units that report to a top leader either directly or indirectly. You not only should be fully aware of your responsibilities to each of these sites, but also should find out how best to communicate with each one. Neglecting field operations is a common leadership problem. It is easy for the leader to get caught up in a combination of corporate business matters at headquarters and in various outreach responsibilities. A good general rule is to spend a disproportionate amount of time with field organizations to demonstrate your involvement, interest, and respect, as well as to update these organizations on your concerns and your changes in policy and plans.

Among the leaders in the organization, what is the standard of integrity? Without constant nurturing, high ethical standards can rapidly deteriorate; one breach of institutional standards quickly leads to another and another. It is essential that you identify the organization's standards of integrity and confirm that they are being practiced by *all*. Review the reporting and inspection systems to ensure that they reinforce, rather than undermine, integrity.

What are the various standards of discipline? It is reasonably easy to ascertain whether deadlines are being met, if products are of high quality, and if overall performance is acceptable. You should look carefully at the performance records of subordinate organizations and staff agencies, to ensure that standards are being met and, when they are not, that prompt, appropriate action is taken.

What documents should I read and in what order? Plans, policy statements, and organizational histories (if available) are fine places to start your reading program. Reading the organization's newsletters or newspapers from the previous few months also can be very helpful, for they will highlight areas of concern. Your deputy or assistant should help prepare this list of documents for you, prioritizing the literature so that you can read the important pieces first.

Is there anything that, if made public, could embarrass my predecessor, the organization, or me? Are there festering problems that are just waiting to jump up and bite me? In other words, are there "skeletons" and, if so, in what closet? It is important to ascertain if there are key individuals in the organization who have serious health problems, including alcoholism, drug abuse, and psychiatric difficulties. Research whether the reporting procedures for harassment are working and working well. Furthermore, confirm that women and minority groups trust these procedures and the people to whom problems would be reported. It is useful to root out institutional "skeletons in the closet" that may not have been revealed in normal reporting for fear that the organization or the boss would look bad, or that corporate credibility would suffer.

What is the overall size of the organization that I am about to lead? Is the present organizational structure effective, and is it, at the same time, encouraging initiative and innovation? The new leader needs to dig into issues of organizational effectiveness to ensure that there is a workable span of control without too many people reporting directly to the leader. As you examine the structural set-up, become aware not only of the present effect on productivity, but also of potential effects to come. Initiative and innovation must be tapped, for these will determine the future success of the organization. You may need to implement changes to the organizational structure that will allow for positive change to occur.

After addressing all of these questions, you should assess the performance of the organization and its ability to accomplish its mission. Your boss and his or her key staff directors can be very helpful, and considerable time should be spent reading the reports of and talking to auditors, inspectors, and evaluators. It is quite common to find that an organization has an inflated view of its own level of performance. Although more unusual, there are organizations that have deflated views of themselves. It is important to walk into a job with an objective understanding of both the perceptions and the realities; thorough assessment is vital. For the conscientious leader, this process never ends.

You will gain valuable knowledge by taking an objective look at the individual who you are replacing. If the organization is in great shape and your predecessor has been a popular leader, it may be worthwhile to continue past policies, to let everybody know that you are honored to follow someone of such stature, and to articulate your hope that you will be able to keep the performance and morale at high levels. If the individual was very popular, but the performance of the organization has been fairly low, you have a greater challenge. You must be willing to demand higher performance levels without denigrating the previous leader. If you are following an individual who was very cold, harsh, or unpopular, but the organization has been functioning well, then your task is easy. By reaching out to people, by thanking and complimenting them often, and by being approachable, you can lift performance even higher by enhancing morale. Finally, if you take over an organization that is not attaining expected results, you can communicate that it is time for everyone in the organization to chart a new course, to recognize the deficiencies that have been preventing optimal achievement, and to work together to upgrade performance at all levels.

It is useful to find out if subordinate leaders have regular counselling sessions with the people who work under them, and if poor performance is being identified, documented, and corrected. The continuity of the organization over the next few years is another important topic; you should look at projections and plans, so that scheduled retirements and other departures of key subordinates can be identified, and so that replacements can be recruited well in advance. Also, younger officials will look to you to establish a promotion system that will give them opportunities for upward mobility.

Decision-making is a critical subject that must be tackled from the very beginning of your new position. Two common decision-making problems should be discussed with associates during the initial phases of the transition process: the "oh, by the way" problem and the "nonconcurrence through silence" issue.

By discussing these matters with your key staff personnel and the subordinate leaders, you can help them to understand and support some important ground rules.

The "oh, by the way" problem is a common phenomenon in most large organizations. At the end of a scheduled meeting, sometimes an associate will approach the leader and say, "Oh, by the way, I would like to raise a new issue and get your decision." Immediately, you should be cautious, since an appropriate answer often requires coordination and a quick decision can be a mistake. A useful way to handle this situation is to listen carefully, ask the individual to coordinate the matter with other staff and field agencies, and to decline the opportunity to make a decision (even a tentative decision) prior to the completion of the coordination process. Sometimes this requires extraordinary self-discipline on the part of the leader, as the associate may be pushing hard for a quick decision. Although there may be some urgency involved and you do not want to appear indecisive, exercise caution and patience. In many cases, a fast decision leads to bad results that will come back to haunt you.

One rule that may be worth establishing is having associates raise the "oh, by the way"s *before* scheduled staff meetings, rather than after them. In this way, you may choose to discuss the topic during the meeting or, if the issue is important or urgent enough, to call a special meeting immediately following the scheduled one. Of course, "oh, by the way"s can come up at almost any time—at lunch, on the tennis court, at the bar, on a trip, etc. You should be receptive to new ideas, but should be very careful in your response. For instance, even the reply, "That sounds OK in principle," might cause an aggressive associate to race off and do something that may cause your organization great grief.

You also may wish to establish a "no nonconcurrence through silence" rule. This was Dwight Eisenhower's number one rule of leadership. Associates who do not concur with the decisions being made in meetings and discussions must understand that they have a responsibility to speak up. By remaining silent during these discussions, they do the leader a grave disservice. A major part of the associates' duties is to speak out on issues, particularly when they disagree with either the context or the thrust of the discussion in which a decision is being made. You should create a decision-making environment in which subordinate associates feel free to express concerns, to raise new options, and to disagree. One useful way to draw out comments from the more introverted associates is to ask the views of specific individuals—call on them by name—who have not spoken up during the discussion.

To be an effective leader, you must work hard to avoid "group-think"—a situation in which there is too much compatibility and a consensus is found too quickly. False consensus, excessive conformity, and group-think are not in the interest of any large organization. Even though some of the concerns raised by associates may be parochial or ill-conceived, the leader must be willing to listen carefully before a final decision is made. There is a direct relationship between the thoroughness and openness of the decision-making process and the effectiveness of the implementation process. If associates are given a full opportunity to express their views prior to the making of the decision, they will be more willing to carry out the decision after it is made, even though it may not be the one that they would have chosen.

You cannot underestimate the advantages of a well-planned transition into leadership. A leader who has gone through the transition process carefully and systematically and knows what he or she wants to do, when to do it, how to make decisions, and how to approach issues, can quickly get the attention and respect of coworkers. A successful transition can make a big difference in both the future performance and the self-esteem of the organization. If the new leader creates an atmosphere that encourages and validates high integrity, planning, and the presentation of contrary views, the organization soon can become a model for others to emulate.

After you have been in charge for two or three months, write a philosophy letter. Using your own words, state the goals and priorities of the organization, as well as particular points of emphasis that are important to you. This letter can serve many useful purposes. It can let everyone know that you are in charge and that you have a good grasp of the organization, have established clear and understandable goals, and have laid out areas of concentration. The letter, in draft form, should be circulated among key subordinate associates for comments and criticism. It is important that they be comfortable with the letter, since they will be responsible for supporting both the goals and the underlying philosophy. The contents should be summarized in the company, university, or post newspaper, and the letter itself should be widely circulated both in hard copy and by e-mail. It should be given to all perspective new employees so that, at an early date, they can understand and identify with both the organization and the leader.

Specific points that may be useful to outline in the philosophy letter include: the rich and successful history of the organization; the commitment to internal and community goals; the need for high personal and institutional integrity; the strategic vision of the leader and the organization; the policy of decentralization and empowerment of subordinate leaders; the seeking of diversity; the need for innovation; and the process whereby creative ideas are advanced. The letter should be brief (no more than two pages), up-beat, and non-threatening, and it should clearly reflect your thoughts and dreams for the organization.

By forcing yourself to write this letter within three months of taking over, you make the important psychological leap from being the new boss to being the person fully in charge. After you have been in charge for about a year, review the letter, revise it, and rewrite it as necessary to reflect any changes in your vision, goals, and philosophy of leadership. A professionally constructed videotape can be another powerful way to communicate. It should be reviewed and updated, if necessary, at least once a year.

3

ESTABLISHING STANDARDS

personal and institutional integrity

There is no pillow so soft as a clear conscience.

—French Proverb

God brings men into deep waters, not to drown them but to cleanse them.

—Aughery

Upon taking over the leadership of an organization, it is vital that you make clear the organization's standards of integrity. One way to do that is through the company newspaper or a newsletter, where you can write down precisely what you mean by integrity and what principles are to be established and maintained. You should also discuss integrity at shop get-togethers, at staff meetings, with subordinate leaders, during speeches, and at award and recognition ceremonies. In the process of writing and talking about integrity, the use of examples from personal experience can be especially effective.

Early in your tenure, you should look for opportunities to demonstrate, within the context of the organization which you now lead, your commitment to integrity. A brief personal example of mine offers a good illustration of this point. At Bitburg, Germany, we were conducting a NATO air defense exercise. My intelligence officer got up in front of all the pilots to outline the reporting guidelines. He asked the pilots to report, on every mission, that they had expended four missiles and half of the bullets from the Gatling gun. He also asked each pilot to report that he had shot down four enemy aircraft. I jumped out of my chair and interrupted the intelligence officer. I said to the pilots, "We will not do that; I don't want to set an example, even in an exercise, of dishonest reporting. What I want you to do is go up, intercept the inbound aggressor airplanes, make your simulated attacks, and report what you *actually* accomplish. If you shoot down four airplanes in simulated combat, report four airplanes destroyed. If you intercept no airplanes, report no airplanes destroyed. Don't falsify reports just to exercise the system." It was a fine opportunity for me to demonstrate that we would not set a pattern of prevarication in our day-to-day activities. I strongly emphasized that whenever you report anything, you should do it honestly and fairly.

Babe Didrikson-Zaharias, who was a great athlete in the 1932 Olympics, became a very successful professional golfer. While playing in a tournament on a golf tour, she noticed that she somehow had played the wrong ball. When the round was over, she penalized herself two strokes, which cost her first place in the tournament. Later, in a quiet conversation, one of her friends asked her, "Babe, why did you do that? No one would have known that you used the wrong ball." Babe answered, "Don't you understand—*I* would have known."

It is this kind of personal integrity that we need to emphasize in all institutions and organizations—a personal commitment to integrity that is deep and profound. In combination with strong commitment to institutional or corporate integrity, this personal strength of character is what leaders should stress and stress frequently. There are people who would never lie in their personal lives, but who would lie for their institution. Yet institutional integrity is just as important, and in some cases more important, than personal integrity. Low levels of institutional integrity damage the credibility of the organization, your own credibility, personal trust, and mutual respect.

Another aspect of integrity to consider is "protecting your signature." Since many of the letters, memoranda, staff papers, messages, regulations, and directives that you sign will be prepared by members of your staff, you should do an "integrity check" before signing the paper. From my experience, the most common violation of integrity is in the personnel system. The general who states that "this is the best lieutenant colonel working for me" can do this only about once a year, or else he undermines his credibility within the personnel and promotion system. There is a great irony in this area. By pushing too many people too hard, a leader hurts all of them because his or her signature and endorsement lose value. In fact, sometimes his or her endorsement becomes a negative factor when the promotion board meets.

An insidious, but very common, breach of integrity occurs when employees are excessively burdened with the task of reporting trivial accomplishments. Often employees will certify the accomplishment of something without actually doing the work. They justify this violation of integrity by saying, "No one will know and no one will care," or "This is a dumb requirement." A useful approach is to initiate action to change the requirement to something much more reasonable. Be sensitive to these overly bureaucratic requirements and personally find out what reports the organization is requiring that tend to be falsified.

Let me give an example to demonstrate my point. Years ago, a large federal government agency required that every sedan be given a daily 30-point inspection by the first driver of the day. This complete bumper-to-bumper inspection, if done properly, took at least an hour to accomplish. In practice, most drivers would sign off the report without inspecting anything. Under more enlightened leadership, the agency changed the inspection system. The new system requires that only one part of the vehicle be examined each day by the person who is assigned to drive it first. If the car has not been driven for the last couple of days, the driver inspects three things. By the end of the month, everything will have been checked once—from battery cables to tire pressure, to oil level, to headlights. Drivers are perfectly willing to spend two or three minutes checking one or two systems. Integrity has returned to the reporting system, and safety has not been compromised.

You should evaluate the moral dimensions of the organization's mission. If the mission ultimately is based on individual worth, human equality, and human dignity, you cannot afford to ignore these values in daily practice. For example, treating people unfairly or allowing unfair treatment to occur in the organization is inconsistent with the values which give that organization its fundamental worth.

Integrity is not something that can be put on and taken off as we go to and from work. People whose character is weak while outside of the job do not have the character required to be leaders. For instance, an individual who engages in spouse or child abuse, falsifies expense account records, cheats on income tax forms, or even cheats at golf is also likely to violate standards of institutional integrity at work. When such a person is placed in a leadership position, the final result often is either short-term or long-term failure; when at the top, he or she will do serious damage to the organization or the institution.

Senior executives, more so than junior leaders, need to be prepared to say "no" when ethics demand. Ethical decisions become ever more complex as individuals grow in power, prestige, and rank. Good moral values will sometimes be in conflict. You must apply ethics with wisdom and maturity. This may be the greatest challenge and the greatest opportunity for the enlightened leader.

People of character and integrity should seek to improve themselves as they move to higher and higher positions of responsibility. Unfortunately, the opposite often occurs. As individuals climb up the slippery pole to success, they often sell their souls incrementally, making small compromises to their personal integrity in order to serve their ambitions or their egos. Junior executives who say to themselves, "I will never be like my dishonest or manipulative boss when I reach the top," too often find themselves at the top, fifteen or twenty years later, acting very much like that boss of the past.

Ambitious leaders and associates often lose sight of the functional nature of high integrity. Honesty *pays*, in so many ways: it gives you and your employees high self-esteem; honestly reporting on your problems helps to get attention and support; it enhances consistency in purpose and execution. On the other hand, falsification leads people in all kinds of unfortunate directions. If someone lies a lot or an organization engages in regular falsification of reports and records, it is awfully hard to remember what the truth is. In other words, lying, falsification of reports, and other forms of dissembling are not only ethically wrong, but also dysfunctional. Make the case that honesty is in *everyone's* best interest and you will raise the level of integrity in your organization.

I often recall an especially memorable experience from my six years of working in the Pentagon. The Chief of Staff of the Air Force received a briefing from his staff on the "Program" for the next five years. This Program outlined the staff's collective advice on how funds should be allocated yearly for the upcoming five-year period. The staff had developed the Program in a way that tried to maximize opportunities to get as much as possible of what was needed. Unfortunately, some of the high priorities of the President and the Secretary of Defense were ignored, or at least circumvented. When the briefing was completed, the Chief of Staff said quietly, but firmly, "This is a dishonest Program; I will not submit it to the Secretary of Defense." The staff was "gaming" the Program, and the Chief of Staff, being faithful to the letter and the spirit of the guidance that he had received from the Secretary of Defense, was unwilling to sign the document. A few weeks later, the Air Force submitted an honest, nonmanipulative program. All of us were uplifted.

Many issues of integrity in the highly politicized atmosphere of Washington, DC are complex and fuzzy. Too often, people take the manipulative road and integrity suffers. Considering the disturbing number of public officials being indicted for their violation of the public trust, a wise observer of the Washington scene has said that what the American people are looking for in their political leaders is *cleanliness*. Perhaps the self-corrective nature of the American political system will lead to increased bipartisanship in foreign policy and to higher levels of integrity in our public servants. Let's hope so. All leaders in government periodically should remind themselves of Grover Cleveland's candid comment, "Public office is a public trust."

The Wall Street scandals of the 1980s and 1990s vividly demonstrate the cost of low integrity to individuals, to their firms, and to the institutions they represent. The importance of business ethics may not be as obvious or as immediately pressing as ethics in government, but it is not an inconsequential factor in the long-term health of Western capitalistic systems. George Washington perhaps said it best when he advised, "Labor to keep alive in your breast that little spark of celestial fire called conscience."

I would like to reemphasize a fundamental point about leadership. Of all the various dimensions of leadership that must be mastered by those who strive to be great leaders, integrity is the most important. I have found great solace and support in reading and rereading the following wonderful books: *The Power of Ethical Management* by Kenneth H. Blanchard and Norman Vincent Peale; *The Nightingale's Song* by Robert Timberg; *Integrity* by Stephen L. Carter; and *How Good People Make Tough Choices* by Rushworth M. Kidder.

4
ORGANIZING PRIORITIES
the mission, the mission the mission

The best leaders are passionate about the mission.
— *Reuben Harris*

The secret of success is constancy of purpose.
— *Disraeli*

There is a slogan in real estate that there are three very important considerations when buying property: location, location, and location. For leaders of organizations, it's the mission, the mission, the mission. If the leader is spending too much time on peripheral issues, and if he or she does not encourage key associates to focus on the accomplishment of the organization's goals, the mission will suffer. Leaders of both small and large organizations tend to have their attention diverted by the unorganized and unprioritized demands of their schedules, their in-boxes, and their telephone calls. Only the most disciplined of leaders gain and maintain control of their schedules and priorities.

You must avoid wasting time on unimportant issues. In addition, be particularly careful not to burden associates at all levels with tasks that do not relate to the goals and priorities of the organization. Some leaders get bored with the heavy commitment of time, energy, and emphasis on the organizational mission, and drift off into areas that may be more fun and interesting, but are not directly related to the mission. These leaders often tie up key associates with projects and staff work that divert them from their most important responsibilities. In addition, some followers and subordinate leaders try to divert the attention of the leader away from the mission. Hence, a focused relationship between leader and follower is vital; leaders and followers who reinforce each other contribute massively to the long-term health of any organization. Such reminders as "first things first" and "let's get back to basics" can be helpful in reinforcing this point.

Of course, leaders should not only speak and write about the importance of the mission; they must demonstrate personal involvement, as well. If a leader is a president or dean of a college or university, that leader also should teach classes. Teaching is a good way to maintain an awareness of the bureaucratic and administrative problems that the faculty is facing relating to course preparation, syllabus development, printing plant capabilities, and faculty problems with publishers and guest speakers. If the leader runs a business, he or she should spend a good deal of time on the shop floor—even working occasionally on the production line, if feasible. Again, the hands-on experience is of extreme value in truly understanding needs and tensions. Where applicable and possible, the responsible leader also visits regularly with the night and graveyard shifts. Over all, leaders should conserve the "organizational energy" and do their very best to ensure that there is no one doing work for the sole purpose of making the leader look good, covering up mistakes, or otherwise detracting from the accomplishment of the mission.

One of the paramount requirements of running larger organizations is the leader's constant jousting with the bureaucracy. This will ensure that the organization does not become stagnant, obsolete, or overly rigid in the face of new challenges and opportunities. Whenever I teach leadership at places like CNN, Texas Instruments, and Microsoft, I am impressed by how committed the various leaders are to the fight against the rigidities of bureaucracy. With less than 20 percent of all professionals within large organizations being "innovators," it is both organizational and individual conservatism which can lead to rigid policies. Some individuals tend to be more interested in survival, in staying out of trouble, in avoiding extra work, or in being promoted, than in carrying out the mission in as effective a way as possible.

Unfortunately, even strong innovators often hide their ideas in the bottom drawer of their desks until the organizational climate is just right for them to surface. This provides the leader with a challenge that is significant, but not insurmountable. A climate of trust, which helps the innovators come out of their shells, can help create an atmosphere of excitement and creativity that can have a major impact on the future of the organization. General George C. Marshall and General Henry H. (Hap) Arnold, two of the great leaders during the World War II era, provided, throughout their long and distinguished careers, the climate for the creativity that led to some amazing results.

George Marshall's commitment to planning, his knowledge of where the truly talented and innovative young professionals were, and his willingness to hire, nurture, and reward them played a vital role in the success of the United States during World War II. The dynamic planning that was done just prior to World War II helped ensure the achievements of the Army and the Army Air Corps. Marshall's commitment to creativity played an important role in the establishment of a separate Air Force, the development of the Marshall Plan, and the significant strategic planning efforts in the War and State Departments in the 1940s. As both a military and civilian government leader, Marshall was absolutely superb—without peer in his time—in creating an atmosphere of high integrity, trust, creativity, and a sense of mission in all the organizations he led: the U.S. Army, the Department of State, and the Department of Defense. If you are looking for a model after whom to pattern yourself, George Marshall would be my recommendation.

Hap Arnold also had a strong commitment to planning and innovation. By the summer of 1943, he had created a post-war planning division that focused its full attention on the challenges and opportunities of the post-war world. He also created the RAND Corporation shortly after World War II. This was an important and innovative step. RAND soon became a model research agency where high-quality, policy-relevant, and, most importantly, interdisciplinary research was accomplished. The creation of RAND and its impact on planning and policy-making in the Air Force is historically unique. It set the pattern for many similar research groups which support governmental organizations or institutions.

In addition to Marshall and Arnold, I have a number of other people on my personal list of role models: Colin Powell; Larraine Matusak, who developed the best leadership development program in the United States—the Kellogg Foundation Leadership Program; Tom Johnson; Gail Evans and Judy Milestone of CNN; and Bill Cunningham, who headed Focus Hope in Detroit, Michigan, until his untimely death in 1997.

Career patterns within large civilian and governmental organizations often encourage superficiality and dilettantism as individuals move rapidly from one job to the next. Within the last twenty years, it has become a complimentary phrase when someone asks, "Can't you hold a job?" What this often means is that some individuals are so bright and successful that they are being moved onward and upward with great rapidity. However, when these individuals reach top leadership positions, they have become so accustomed to holding jobs for only one or two years that they often neglect to dig deeply into organizational issues. As a result, they sometimes fail as leaders. Their time horizons have been habitually short, and tendencies toward superficiality are increased by too many job changes.

The transition from follower to leader and from leader of a small organization to leader of a large one is, for many, a difficult one. Work patterns, peer relationships, time management, knowledge of details, generating candid feedback, and a myriad of other things change significantly when, at last, you get the chance to be a boss. Leaders must focus a considerable amount of their attention on the mission of the organization and not allow themselves to be diverted by the unprioritized demands of their telephone calls, their in-boxes, or their meeting and travel schedules. Subordinate leaders often have little choice but to follow a schedule which they have limited control over. However,

leaders of large organizations, if they choose to do so, can structure their own schedules to a considerable degree. Yet, too many
leaders (who for years had little control) refuse to grab the bull
by the horns and establish their *own* schedule and their *own* set
of priorities which will serve the mission best.

The best leaders set their own priorities, but place *mission*
first. They periodically check on how they are spending their
time and their energies. They ask themselves what their own
"hidden agendas" are and how closely those agendas conform to
the accomplishment of the mission. Since so much of mission
accomplishment relates to the morale, effectiveness, and performance of key subordinates, the leader should spend a considerable amount of time nourishing leader-follower relationships.

When you are selected to lead a large organization, this
new challenge should be approached with a very different
mindset than is appropriate when you are selected for a staff or
lower-level leadership position. Top leaders must have longer
time horizons, must be willing to empower associates with the
authority to make and implement important decisions, and
must be generous in giving credit to associates for their ideas,
energies, and sense of mission. Big leaders who do not develop
this mindset may be good caretakers, gatekeepers, or managers,
but are unlikely to be leaders who will make the kind of changes
that will take their organizations in important new directions or
lead to dramatically enhanced levels of mission accomplishment.

If you are a leader of a large organization, you must realize
that most of your associates want you to succeed, but a few will
want you to fail. Most will carry out your guidance with enthusiasm and skill. Conversely, some will work against this guidance, in hopes of undercutting your initiatives. In large organizations, there will be individuals who tend to resist initiatives
that are not their own ideas. Strive to capture the imagination
and support of associates by encouraging them to come up with
new concepts. It is a wise leader, indeed, who listens carefully to
associates and helps to turn their best ideas into organizational
initiatives.

Great leaders exercise humility regularly and often. In fact, it is the sign of a great leader never to take personal credit for the success of the organization. Self-aggrandizement is a counter-productive quality. The leader who gets up in front of any group and states that the organization that he or she has led for the last two years was initially in terrible shape, but is in wonderful shape today, reveals a great deal. An objective observer would conclude that the organization was probably not as bad as this leader says it was two years ago, and not as good as he or she is proclaiming it to be today. The truly mature leader will most likely say that the organization was in fine shape on arrival and any improvements that have taken place are the result of the talents and hard work of associates.

It is wise for a leader of a large organization to consider the point that Henry Kissinger made many years ago in his book, *The Necessity for Choice:* "One of the paradoxes of an increasingly specialized, bureaucratized society is that the qualities required in the rise to eminence are less and less the qualities required once eminence is reached." A question that a leader should often ask associates is, "How can I help you, and how can I make your job easier?" A related question is, "What am I doing that is making your job difficult, and what is it about my style or decisions that really bothers you?" If leaders don't ask these kinds of questions periodically, they are liable to become part of the problem rather than part of the solution. You may think you are doing a great job, while, in fact, other people may be spending a great deal of their time picking up after you or trying to reduce the impact of the mistakes that you are making.

A leader of larger organizations should not only know what is happening within the organization and have solid operational and technical competence, but should avoid spending a great deal of time in the details of the decisions. Someone once suggested that when Jimmy Carter was President, he didn't look at the forest and didn't look at the trees, but spent all his time looking at the leaves on the trees. This tendency toward micromanagement should be avoided scrupulously. Micromanagement, coupled with inconsistency, can be deadly. Often ask yourself: "Am I consistent in supporting the priorities which I have established, or am I constantly confusing and frustrating people?"

There is a fundamental paradox that all leaders must understand and tackle as best as they can: the bigger the organization, the more trust that is required, yet the harder it is to engender and reinforce trust. Leaders must not only trust associates, they must believe in their own competence.

A major problem in many organizations is a distorted notion of mission that some leaders and associates have. Some people will justify doing stupid, immoral, or illegal things in order to "accomplish the mission." But the mission of an organization cannot be separated from the values and principles upon which that organization is built. If an associate tries to justify using illegal or immoral means to accomplish a legal or moral mission, the leader must remind him or her that there should be a direct relationship between ends and means, and that both must be of high integrity. This may be one of the major enduring lessons of the various scandals which have plagued the American Presidency in recent decades.

I have found that *negative* role models can be extremely helpful in educating an aspiring leader. When I served my first tour in the Pentagon, I worked for a general officer who was extremely hard-working and very ambitious, but quite insecure, had a poor sense for policy issues, and was not very smart. Over one hundred officers worked hard to keep him out of trouble with his bosses. We failed. After a year, he was fired. He made almost every mistake in the book. During this agonizing time, I observed him closely and tried to learn from his mistakes. He taught me a great deal about what not to do and how not to do it. His negative example served me well when I moved into leadership positions. History has given us a number of useful negative role models to study. My favorites include: Robert McNamara; George McClellan; and Warren Harding. H.R. McMaster's book, *Dereliction of Duty: Lyndon Johnson, Robert McNamara and the Joint Chiefs of Staff and the Lies That Led to Vietnam* highlights McNamara's faults brilliantly. McNamara, the Secretary of Defense during much of the Vietnam War, was bright, focused, and analytical, but he suffered from three major faults: incompetence as a strategist, fundamental dishonesty, and arrogance. In my mind, he was not only the worst American public servant of the twentieth century, but also did more damage and spilled more blood than any other American of his time.

A leader must be loyal to the boss, the mission, the people, the organization, the nation, and, in some cases, to a supranational or international organization such as NATO, the Organization of American States, or the United Nations. Keeping these loyalties in proper perspective is a very important aspect of mature leadership. Almost everyone has a boss, and although leaders of some organizations have a great deal of autonomy, both in policy-making and in geographic span, they still must answer to someone, whether it be to their chief executive officers, a board of directors, the stockholders, the U.S. Congress, or the American people. Elbert Hubbard's remarks ring true on the issue of loyalty: "Remember this. If you work for a man, in heaven's name, work for him. If he pays you wages which supply you bread and butter, work for him; speak well of him; stand by him and stand by the institution he represents. If put to a pinch, an ounce of loyalty is worth a pound of cleverness. If you must vilify, condemn and eternally disparage— resign your position, and when you are on the outside, damn to your heart's content, but as long as you are part of the institution, do not condemn it."

Keeping an eye on the goals and making sure that priorities stay in order are not always easy tasks for a leader. For those in public service, the West Point motto is a useful guide: "Duty, Honor, Country." A public servant must be willing to resign if these fundamental principles cannot be upheld. By staying focused on the mission, leaders at all levels can make a huge difference in the success of their organizations.

5
TAKING CARE OF YOUR PEOPLE
mentoring, not cronyism

It is one of the most beautiful compensations of this life that no man can sincerely try to help another without helping himself.
—Ralph Waldo Emerson

Help those around you all you can. Every bit of help you give others will come back to you tenfold.
—E.B. Gallaher

A vital role of the leader is that of ensuring that associates are rewarded properly and moved on to subsequent and more senior assignments in a deliberate and thoughtful way. You should identify the very best associates, monitor their careers, encourage the reaching of their potential, and help them attain promotions within the organization.

On the other hand, be very careful not to fall into the trap of cronyism. A leader who pushes "his boys" or "her girls" often causes morale problems. Practicing cronyism also can hurt the very people you are trying to help. If you push a person into a big job before he or she is capable of handling it, or force a protégé on a subordinate leader, you often do that individual a great disservice. And if the subordinate leader really does not want the protégé, it is very likely that the latter's career will suffer in the long run.

The handling of flatterers and bootlickers is an issue related to cronyism. In all large organizations, there are individuals who are very skillful in pleasing the boss by bearing good news and by stroking the boss's ego. They are always looking for ways to make the boss happy, worrying about getting a lot of "face time" with the boss, and serving their personal ambitions. Unfortunately, there is a direct relationship between cronyism and bootlicking. Leaders must be sensitive to this significant problem area. A good rule of thumb for dealing with sycophants is to give them some counselling and then send them off to a job that takes them away from the corporate headquarters.

As a leader, you should pay particular attention to the "late bloomer." Within every organization, there are people of enormous talent who have matured later in life than their contemporaries. The late bloomer needs particular attention since personnel managers generally tend to overlook their career potential because this potential was not evident earlier.

A number of dysfunctional qualities sometimes develop in very talented people. The first dysfunctional quality is arrogance. No matter how talented an individual may be, if he or she becomes very arrogant, this person will be unlikely to succeed over the long term as a leader. Additionally, many individuals who exhibit potential early in their career do not live up to expectations. Leaders who are sponsoring individuals should periodically look at them with a critical eye to be sure that these associates are not dealing with demands that are beyond their capabilities. A helpful guideline is the "one-push rule": give these individuals one strong upward push and then leave them alone. Associates who have truly outstanding talent and potential will keep moving upward with no additional help from you. And regarding those who have reached their ultimate level of potential and competence, further sponsoring them toward higher positions is a mistake. In a comprehensive analysis of why extremely competent young executives get "derailed" on the way to the top, the Center for Creative Leadership in Greensboro, North Carolina, has reported that "overmentoring" often hurts these high achievers.

Many leaders make the mistake of confining their mentoring to those on the executive track. Mentorship also consists of identifying the best of the people at the lowest level and giving them a compliment and a boost. You must ensure that the organization is not neglecting or abusing the associates at lower levels—the people with the least power. You should consider establishing a formal mentoring program so that certain associates don't get left without a mentor. Racial and gender minorities especially will appreciate the care and support received from their mentors.

George Marshall probably provides the best model in the area of constructive mentoring. He had identified people of great talent and potential during the first thirty-five years of his Army career. Marshall had a carefully compiled list of outstanding people in the Army and Army Air Corps. When President Franklin Delano Roosevelt selected him to be the Chief of Staff of the Army in 1939, Marshall used this list when selecting individuals for key staff and command positions in the immediate pre-war period. When war broke out, he further used this list extensively to pick the top wartime leaders. To a very large extent, the U.S. military did extremely well in World War II because of General Marshall's prudent sponsorship of people of talent, character, and leadership potential.

On the other hand, leaders should not bring a substantial number of former colleagues with them when they move to new positions. A leader who drags a coterie of "the old gang" to the new job is likely to undermine the morale of the new organization. It also will be difficult to develop good rapport with new associates, and communication channels will be harder to establish. In addition, you will gain more credibility as a person of self-confidence and independent thought if you do not drag along with you a group of cronies as you move from job to job.

Finally, leaders of large organizations should provide guidance to subordinate leaders and personnel managers concerning the criteria for promotion. The promotion system must be not only fair, but also perceived to be so. Select members of promotion panels or boards very carefully. Then give specific written guidance to each of them. Also, prior to the time when it convenes, meet privately with the head of the promotion board. After the board completes its work, the head should report back to the leader and state specifically where the board was unable to carry out its guidance completely. Appendix A includes a useful checklist for promotion boards. (See Checklist #21.) It is a modified version of a checklist that was developed by Admiral J. S. Gracey, former Commandant of the United States Coast Guard.

I cannot end this chapter on assisting and mentoring others without sharing one of my favorite quotes. Ruth Smeltzer states, "You have not lived a perfect day . . . unless you have done something for someone who will never repay you."

6

DECENTRALIZING AND GETTING FEEDBACK
a twin dilemma

Strange as it sounds, great leaders gain authority by giving it away.

—James Stockdale

It does an organization no good when its leader refuses to share his leadership function with his lieutenants. The more centers of leadership you find in a company, the stronger it will become.

—David Ogilvey

There is a great deal of discussion in the literature on leadership that pertains to centralization versus decentralization. Most well-run organizations have a balanced amount of the two. At each level, there should be a certain amount of decision-making authority and a certain amount of empowerment. The best leaders have a solid grasp of every level of decision-making and authority. They know which decisions should be made at each level and they compliment subordinate leaders for ensuring that decisions are being made at the appropriate levels.

An essential element of the decentralization and delegating process is making sure that associates understand the organizational values, goals, priorities, and the "big picture." This is an ongoing endeavor, with the top executive playing an important role as a teacher who emphasizes and reinforces the organization's standards. Decentralization and delegation do not mean that the top leader becomes invisible or disengaged; they signify that the hand on the tiller is a light one.

It is important for associates at all levels to receive psychic rewards for the work they do, and this can be accomplished through trust in their authority and their decisions. Subordinate leaders should feel responsible and important. With the general trend in America toward better communication and more centralization, all leaders must work tirelessly to push decisions down to the appropriate levels.

A dilemma emerges as a direct result of the marvelous network of communication and the diversity of feedback mechanisms that exist in large modern organizations. The following situation often occurs. A new leader takes over, reorganizes the company to enhance decentralization, articulates a philosophy of the empowerment of subordinate leaders, and establishes some excellent feedback mechanisms. As the feedback loops give the leader lots of information, he or she tends to jump into problem areas or areas of personal interest. Soon the leader is aggressively recentralizing the organization so that he or she can make decisions that subordinate leaders should be making.

How can you strike the proper balance between centralization and decentralization? Learn to accept feedback with equanimity—do not panic—and use the information to stay in touch with employees' concerns and ideas. Thus, you can be helpfully aware, but not fully engaged in decisions at every level. Also, help accomplish your goals by asking your subordinate leaders some key questions; do not spend time struggling to resolve matters that competent staff members can handle. On rare occasions, you may feel that you must jump into an issue or problem personally. When you do decide to get directly involved, work closely with the subordinate leaders who normally have responsibility for this area. Thus, they will not feel disregarded or incapable, and they will gain valuable skills for the future. As a top leader, you should stay in touch and stay involved, but discipline your tendencies to control and complete what has been assigned to others, or you will slide down the slippery slope of continuous micromanagement. It is important to realize that micromanagement—the compulsive inclination to get into an infinite number of unimportant details—is seldom productive for leaders.

Within the context of an organization that has the proper amount of decentralization, the leader must secure a number of effective feedback mechanisms so that he or she can be apprised of important events. The normal hierarchical structure (or chain of command, in the military) that often provides excellent feedback is helpful, but other means are needed to supplement it. An inspection system and an auditing system are methods by which you can attain essential information. You should have a close relationship with both the chief inspector and the auditor. It is important for them to tell the whole and unvarnished truth. The inspection system must be staffed with excellent people who, because of their recognized competence, have the respect of individuals at all levels. It also must emphasize integrity and not deteriorate into a pattern of activity that encourages prevarication and the withholding of important information. Self-inspection systems within subordinate organizations also can be effective tools. You should show interest in and support for such systems and ask for periodic reports on problem areas uncovered by self-inspection.

Management control systems, which allow a great deal of quantifiable data to reach the leader, are also useful feedback mechanisms. However, in their worst forms, they can become heavy burdens, detract from the mission, and deteriorate into data manipulation and dishonest reporting. Do not take for granted that computer access to all kinds of information within the organization is timely or accurate. If the information in the computer system is found to be inaccurate or dishonest, you should shut down the system or take corrective action. The information flow must be restored so that it effectively supports the leading and managing of the organization. The management control system should be examined periodically and in detail by an outside agency, in order to ensure that it truly is serving your needs and those of the mission.

From time to time, executives should delve into reports that staff agencies are submitting to higher headquarters. These reports often bring pressure upon subordinate associates, and there may be temptations to violate integrity. In other words, the documents that go to corporate headquarters, in addition to those that are sent to your attention, may be sources of the breakdown of personal and institutional honesty and character.

Some workers may be inclined to "fudge" numbers or manipulate results. Therefore, be aware that these documents are not foolproof. You may decide to perform occasional, but subtle checks, where possible.

Associates can identify phony and/or problematic leaders very rapidly and, therefore, are an excellent source of insight concerning subordinate leaders working for you. Someone who may look wonderful to you may look very different when viewed from below. Walt Ulmer, who has held many top executive positions and is the former president of the Center for Creative Leadership, feels that there should be some subordinate input into personnel evaluations. Although this may be impracticable in a formal sense, there is a great deal of wisdom in Ulmer's point. Informal mechanisms can be helpful in ensuring that the top leader does not tolerate abysmal leadership on the part of one or more subordinate leaders.

Informal feedback through individuals who are not in the organizational hierarchy and who do not work directly for the top leader can also be effective. Retired associates who are keeping in close touch with friends who remain within the organization can be good sources of mature and objective feedback. The spouses' communication net can provide valuable insights, as well. Additionally, there almost always are "tuned-in" individuals who, although they do not occupy key positions within the hierarchical structure, can be helpful.

Gathering information through informal conversation among friends is an extremely effective feedback technique. A president of a multibillion dollar corporation (and dear friend of mine) told me that the way he stays in touch with the various aspects of his organization is through lots of off-the-record phone calls from friends throughout his company and throughout his industry. This man possesses such extraordinary kindness and thoughtfulness that it is easy to see why he has such a vast network of friends and information. People like him and enjoy staying in contact with him, keeping him informed. His sincere charm and concern allow him to effectively tap into the undercurrents of his business.

Informal means of feedback should be used carefully. As a

leader, you have a responsibility to support subordinate leaders and not to violate the established rules of hierarchy. On the other hand, not utilizing informal means of communication can be a mistake. Without good feedback from many sources, a leader is partially blind and, over time, can become isolated from the real problems and the real issues. Isolation diminishes the ability to anticipate problems, to receive innovative ideas, to maximize opportunities, and to serve as an enlightened and creative leader.

You should be particularly sensitive to feedback from members of groups who may feel, both collectively and individually, that they are "second-class citizens." If not given proper attention, these groups can become a source of poor morale and poor performance. There is a dilemma here; while decentralization works to share power and provide hands-on leadership, it also can lead to neglect of certain groups, including racial and ethnic minorities, maintenance staff, and administrative and clerical personnel. Make a special effort to give members of these groups adequate time, support, and loving care, even though you may be violating, on occasion, the desirable policy of decentralization.

Minorities can bring enormous strength to an organization by providing a diversity of cultural experiences and a certain cohesiveness within each group. Wise leaders know how to maximize the benefits of this strength, always pursuing an enlightened policy toward equal opportunity and fair treatment. As a leader, you should make yourself available to the informal leaders of various minority groups. Through this contact, you will come to understand issues and dynamics of which you otherwise might not have been aware. You also can obtain feedback and valuable ideas from these influential associates. For example, I had 400 African-Americans and approximately 100 Latinos under my command at Bitburg Air Base in Germany. I attended many dinners and preached at numerous religious gospel services during this time. These activities permitted me to stay in touch with two very cohesive and very supportive groups, to hear their feedback and, ultimately, to serve as a better leader.

Periodically, you should remind yourself that the organization's minority groups and individuals are "eternally visible." Admiral Paul Reason, a bright and articulate African-American officer, explains how minority individuals often feel the heat of the spotlight: "If you do something right, everyone will notice; if you do something wrong, everyone will notice." This high visibility tends to put extra pressure on any person who easily can be recognized by skin color or gender. In one sense, all leaders feel this same type of pressure, as they are also "on display." Hence, leaders can "bond" with associates from minority groups because they have this visibility factor in common.

Leaders who are women or who come from racial or ethnic minority groups have an advantage in this general area; it is relatively easy for them to get good feedback from other members of the organization who are of the same gender or heritage. But these leaders face a reverse dilemma; that is, how to ensure that the conventional organizational feedback loops operate effectively. They need to stay in close contact with key associates who are, in turn, in close contact with (or part of) these more traditional loops.

The whole issue of equal opportunity for racial, religious, and ethnic minorities and women will become even more important in the future than it has been in the past. Too many of this country's top leaders, who consider themselves to be quite enlightened, in fact carry deep within them some very heavy prejudices toward one or more of these groups. As you look around the conference table at meetings, observe how many women and members of minority groups are present. An enlightened leader will construct a training and development program that will recruit, train, and promote minorities. Therefore, in the long-term future of the organization, the various cultural elements will be properly represented in the highest positions. A program such as this is not only the right thing to do, but also is functionally sound, for no organization can maximize the vital feedback mechanism if only men from one race sit around the corporate and organizational boardrooms across the globe.

7

MAKING THE BIG
DECISIONS

seven useful checks

In the long run men hit only what they aim at.
　　　　　　　　　　—*Henry David Thoreau*

After all is said and done, there is a lot more said than done.
　　　　　　　　　　　　　—*Anonymous*

From my experience in government and from observing a number of corporations at rather close hand, it is my judgment that most top executives try to make too many decisions. Most decisions should be made at levels below the top; the leaders should dedicate their precious time to the really key or sensitive decisions. It is a wise leader, indeed, who focuses most of his or her attention on the big decisions (a dozen or so each year) and decisions that involve particularly sensitive issues (perhaps another dozen). Generally, if leaders attempt to make a much greater number of decisions, either they are unable to be fully informed on the issues or they are unable to follow up properly to ensure that the implementation process carries out the letter and spirit of the decisions. In other words, if a leader tries to do too much, he or she will, in the long run, accomplish too little.

Before you make a decision, ensure that complete coordination has taken place and that all important players, both inside and outside the organization, have had an opportunity to express fully their views. At any decision-making meeting, you should reemphasize the "no nonconcurrence through silence" rule (pages 23–24). This will draw out the views of quiet skeptics who worry about the direction that you may be taking and can offer some useful cautionary comments about the thrust of your thinking.

There are seven important checks to apply when preparing to make a final decision: the sanity check; the dignity check; the systems check; the *60 Minutes, CNN,* or *Washington Post* check; the safety check; the strategy check; and the integrity check. This seven-check rule of thumb has served me well not only as a leader, but also as a follower and as an adviser to senior executives.

The *sanity check* is very simple, but quite important. Now that the agony of the coordination process is over and now that all of the delicate compromises have been made to get the key agencies and individuals to support the tentative decision, does the decision make sense? Have we created a thoroughbred racehorse, a plodding but sturdy farm horse, or a camel with ten humps? The farm horse may be the best you can get, and you may have to be satisfied with that. But do not accept the camel. If a decision doesn't make sense, it is the obligation of the leader to reject it and to give guidance to the staff on how to proceed. It is not fair to the staff if a rejected but carefully compromised and coordinated decision paper is returned without some guidance on where to proceed.

The *dignity check* is also fundamental and uncomplicated. Will this decision enhance the reputation and dignity of this organization and leadership, or will it undermine that reputation? If the latter is the case—if the decision "smells bad"—you should return the issue for further staff consideration. Furthermore, you should provide subordinates with some "top-down" guidance concerning your objections and offer suggestions on how to fix the problems.

The *systems check* requires a careful consideration of the various parts of the decision to ensure that there is internal consistency and coherency and that this decision also fits within the overall goals of the organization. Even though individual parts of the decision may make sense when analyzed separately, all parts must fit together if the decision is to have any chance of being implemented in a way that will serve the interests of the leader and the organization. An airplane analogy illustrates the need for the compatibility of parts: the wings, fuselage, engines, cockpit, landing gear, and pilot must all fit nicely together or the airplane (the decision) will not fly—or if it does fly, it will not fly smoothly.

The *60 Minutes, CNN, or Washington Post check* involves a straightforward examination of how the decision will appear when it is written up by a media critic. From my many years of work in the Pentagon, I have found this area of discussion to be most useful when it comes to stopping superiors from making foolish decisions. One effective technique is to try to frame a very critical headline and, at the appropriate time, to raise the issue this way: "I can see the headline in the paper next week— 'Department of Defense Decides to Change the Name of the National War College: Curriculum Stays the Same—Still Studying War; Another Example of Defense Department Deception?'" The media receives a lot of criticism and much of it is deserved, but if it wasn't for the media playing its role as watchdog and critic, the number of stupid decisions made in government and elsewhere would increase significantly.

The *safety check* should take in the physical and psychological safety of employees and customers alike. A corporation's products will be used by a large diversity of people. If a product emits low level but dangerous radiation, if long-term use of the product leads to carpal tunnel syndrome, if a drug has side effects that can injure even a few users, or if the food product contains an excessively high level of bacteria, leaders must be aware and get involved. The Valujet crash in 1996 serves as a different but vivid example. If a simple heat and fire detector had been placed in the cargo hold, the airplane would probably have been saved. The pilot would have been alerted and either aborted the takeoff or landed quickly.

The *strategy check* is critical in determining how much a decision will help or hurt the future of the organization. Decisions often make good tactical sense, but fail the strategy check. In the early 1980s, IBM made a decision to attack its personal computer advocates because they were beginning to threaten the corporation's mainframe gurus. As a result, IBM squandered its early edge in personal computer technology and allowed Compaq, Dell, and Apple to gain a large market share. This is an example of the lack of serious strategic focus. As another example, consider Japan's decision to bomb Pearl Harbor. If the Japanese leaders in 1941 had done an objective strategic analysis of the decision to launch that air attack, they might have chosen another course of action. By questioning the key Japanese assumption that the United States would be willing to sue for peace after receiving a devastating sneak attack, strategic leaders might have said, "Now wait just a minute." Japanese leaders should have checked themselves against American history; whenever Americans perceived that they were attacked by foreigners—by the British in 1812, by the Mexicans at the Alamo, by the Spanish when the Battleship Maine was blown up, by the German U boats on the high seas prior to American entry into World War I—the United States always reacted with strong military force. Tojo and the other key Japanese leaders were brilliant tacticians, but terrible strategic thinkers. They failed to conduct an objective strategy check.

The *integrity check* is the basic ethics issue. It concerns both the means and the ends of the decision, as well as the long-term reputation of the organization. In the interest of pursuing legitimate goals, have you selected unethical means to beat the competition, to fool the press, to outsmart the Congress, to beat your bureaucratic foe? Are the goals themselves ethical? The integrity check can be very useful as a deterrent to dishonorable, immoral behavior. If your associates know that you are going to conduct an ethical examination of every issue, they are much more likely to find ethical means to reach ethical ends.

All true leaders are agents of change, as they create a strategic vision and take their organizations to higher levels of performance and excellence. The decision-making process is an important means by which leaders accomplish these goals. To make this element of your leadership most effective, conceptualize your approach to decision-making and make it a systematic process.

Leaders who limit themselves to making only a few decisions each month have the time to check periodically on the coherency and consistency of those decisions. They also are able to reflect upon the important interrelationship between their strategic visions and their decisions. In contrast, leaders who race around to put out fires may get lots of psychic rewards from staying extremely busy, but the price they pay—reduced coherency and weakened leadership vision—is likely to be quite high. As a leader, you should draw satisfaction not from the *quantity* of your decisions, but from their *quality*. Also, train yourself to get satisfaction not only out of the decision itself, but out of its full implementation.

8

SCHEDULING YOUR TIME

disciplining yourself and your calendar

Time is the least thing we have of.
>   —*Ernest Hemingway*

Lost time is never found again.
>   —*Benjamin Franklin*

There has been much research in America on the issue of time management for executives. I have had the opportunity to survey that research. In addition, I have had a chance to observe, at close hand, how executives in corporations, non-profits, and the military manage their time. Having worked directly for an Englishman and for a German in a large international headquarters in Northern Germany, I have gained some additional insights about how leaders from various nations can best schedule and carry out their daily activities.

My British boss, Sir Peter Terry, did not have a daily, weekly, or monthly staff meeting. He interacted with his subordinates through staff papers, informal meetings, and briefings on specific subjects. As an American, I was appalled by this approach of having no scheduled meetings whatsoever. However, I soon learned that this system worked. Instead of spending much of their time in meetings, people were doing productive work. In addition, Terry's leadership style gave me great freedom to make decisions on his behalf, which I greatly appreciated.

My German boss, General Paul Monreal, was also uncomfortable with large staff meetings. He felt that they wasted a lot of time that many people could put to more productive use. My plea for a monthly staff meeting was finally granted, but only after I agreed to discipline the meeting in two ways; the meeting would last no more than an hour, and it would not serve as a vehicle for shortcuts that would lead to quick, but ill-considered decisions. Monreal met privately with me once or twice a week, to philosophize about our mission and to share ideas on some of the better books on history and current issues that related to our mission. It was refreshing, indeed, to work for Monreal and for Terry—two men who cared less about deadlines than they did about substance, and who took the time to think deeply about strategic issues and opportunities.

Dwight D. Eisenhower, who had considerable experience in international organizations prior to his Presidency, had a wonderful sense about where and how decisions should be made. He knew the difference between line and staff activities. He disciplined his in-box by sending numerous decision papers back to the appropriate cabinet or agency head. He would attach short notes to these papers: "This is not a presidential decision; I want you to make this decision." By doing so, he had more time for the truly important or particularly sensitive issues, and for reflection and planning.

Don Rumsfeld, when he was Secretary of Defense, impressed all of us who worked in his outer office with the discipline of his schedule. Each week he would have a meeting dedicated to working out the next week's schedule with his key staff members. Attending the meeting were the Chief of Public Affairs, the Chief of Congressional Relations, Rumsfeld's executive assistant, and, in many cases, the Deputy Secretary of Defense. By developing a carefully planned schedule which he followed quite carefully, Rumsfeld not only disciplined himself, but also helped to discipline the process of decision-making. He scheduled free time each day for contingencies and catch-up time. As a result of his good planning, he almost always stayed on schedule. Officials from throughout the Pentagon did not have to waste time cooling their heels in the outer office, waiting for a meeting to start.

I collected a number of helpful time-saving techniques from a CEO of a large research firm that does technical work for large companies and for the government. He requests that those meetings that he is not chairing begin at 11:00 a.m., rather than 9:00 a.m. or 10:00 a.m., since he knows that many people have luncheon engagements and, hence, will move to the important issues more quickly. When he does chair a meeting, the CEO follows a set pattern, allowing a maximum of one hour for the meeting, and he always announces the purpose of the meeting at the start. If the purpose of the meeting is to reach a decision, he will often say, "In about forty minutes, I am going to ask for your views on a decision concerning the matter at hand." Also, those who do not speak up in a meeting usually are not invited back to the next meeting on the same subject. He feels that if, after a full hour of discussion, certain individuals have nothing at all to contribute, they will probably be wasting company time and money by attending the next meeting. This means that there will be a smaller group in attendance at the next meeting, and smaller groups are generally better at reaching decisions. Although there is a danger of establishing a climate for "groupthink" with this approach, this CEO has found a way to avoid the problem; he always ensures that there are one or two strong "devil's advocates" present at all decision meetings. Yet another time-management technique that he uses is to time the length of his telephone calls. Any associate who speaks to him for more than fifteen minutes on more than one or two occasions is counselled quietly about being too long-winded.

There are many useful time-management skills that you can develop as you move up the ladder, so that when you finally take the "big job," you will be well-prepared. For example, an effective leader knows how to dictate clearly. Teddy Roosevelt was able to dictate as many as twenty-five letters per hour. (He would alternate back and forth between two secretaries.) He was able to complete most of a full day's work in a couple of hours through this dictation method. In the past, fast and efficient dictation required a secretary who took dictation well. However, voice recognition software is now available, so that leaders can talk directly to their computers. Hence, dictation, once a dying art, has made a significant comeback.

Another aspect of managing time is speed reading. Time can be better utilized if a leader can read very fast and rapidly find the essence of issues. A speed reading course, or just practicing your reading, is very helpful. In addition, there is speed-reading software available for those leaders who use computers and e-mail extensively. If you can get through an in-box in an hour or two (whereas it might take slower readers a full day), you will have more time to be out with your people, to have substantive meetings on important issues, and to be a true leader, rather than just a desk manager.

The maximum use of secretaries, administrative and special assistants, and deputies is also a significant part of effective time management. Careful recruiting, testing, and hiring of these staff members is vitally important. A good secretary can help you maintain an efficient calendar that reflects how you want to spend your day. You and your secretary should work carefully to design a weekly and monthly schedule that fits your time clock, your body rhythms, and your priorities.

Maintaining "open time" every day is a helpful idea. This time should be set aside for thinking, handling crises, seeing unexpected visitors, or dealing with fast-moving issues. If commitments fill your calendar at 15- or 30-minute intervals from 7:30 a.m. until 6:00 p.m., you are managing your time poorly. You probably are getting into too much detail and not allowing yourself to think and plan. Moreover, associates who really need to see you on short notice may not be able to reach you promptly.

As a general rule, you should not schedule more than one event per hour. Furthermore, your schedule should allow open time between meetings and events. Use this time to return phone calls, to work on items in your in-box, and to think and prepare for the next commitment. It is a reality of leading a large organization that there are increasing demands on your time. More and more people want and need to see you. Organizational priorities and your own priorities come into conflict. Work smarter, not harder; learn to say "no" to time-wasters. Thus, you will be able to deal more efficiently with the "pathology of information" and information overload. The key is to understand that, as the leader, you have the authority to manage your time, but it takes work, a disciplined outer office, a tough-minded attitude, and good planning.

9

REACHING OUTWARD AND UPWARD

building bridges and braintrusts

*A man should live with his superiors as he does with his fire;
not too near, lest he burn, nor too far off, lest he freeze.*

—*Diogenes*

*We must all hang together, or assuredly we shall all hang
separately.*

—*Benjamin Franklin*

It is important for the leader of a large organization not only to
know his or her people and mission well, to plan carefully, and
to manage the solution of problems, but also to reach out to
other organizations and groups. Effective leadership involves
contact with higher headquarters, sister units, the outside community, and institutions with whom the organization has
important interactions. A leader should spend a considerable
amount of time building bridges.

A useful formula to be followed is to treat sister organizations with warmth, respect, and affection. Permitting or encouraging "turf battles" with neighboring institutions does the
organization no good. If the top leader figuratively embraces the
leaders of bureaucratic rivals and lets everyone in the organization know that destructive criticism, backbiting, and turf battles
will not be tolerated, many of the problems that exist between
organizations will disappear quickly. This is true whether the
"rivalry" is between a mayor and the city council; between two
production facilities in a manufacturing company; between the
branch offices of an international bank; between the planners

and the programmers; between the Governor's office and the State Assembly; or between the Department of Defense and the Department of State. When a leader pledges to work cooperatively, he or she considerably reduces the risk of highly competitive individuals turning good, honest competition into dysfunctional criticism, parochialism, and unproductive opposition.

In working with higher headquarters, be sure to remain loyal to those above you, knowledgeable concerning the key agencies and department heads, and cooperative with the staff members. However, you must keep an eye on staff members and departments or agencies at headquarters that ask unreasonable things of your people, put unwarranted pressures on your organization, and operate as if they were the ultimate leaders. It is important for the leader of a lower-level organization to stand up for his or her people, to contact the associates who are placing undue requirements on them, and to set standards for interaction that are appropriate within the organizational hierarchy or chain of command. Doing this delicately and with mutual respect is a difficult job, but one which must be tackled. It has been my experience that senior executives want to know how well their staff and subordinate organizations are working together. When leaders call attention to problem areas in a diplomatic way and make appropriate suggestions for improvement through the chain of command, higher headquarters will be responsive and, in fact, appreciative of the input.

At the higher levels of large organizations, outreach becomes almost an art form. The chemistry that develops between you, as a leader, and your boss greatly affects the relationship between your staff, your boss's staff, and your subordinate organizations. If you can maintain an atmosphere of mutual trust and respect between you and your boss, as well as with top staff people, your associates will benefit. Of course, trust and good chemistry are fairly easy to establish and maintain when your organization performs most of its duties, tasks, and missions in an outstanding way. If, however, the chemistry between you and your boss is bad—or if his or her staff is constantly "poisoning your well"—you and your associates are in for a rough time. As leader, it is your responsibility to nurture good chemistry and ease tensions between your organization and the higher echelon.

Part of your role as a leader is to instruct your associates not to fight with higher headquarters and staff agencies, but to cooperate with them. If there is a battle to be waged, gather the facts and engage in the battle yourself. In addition, do not forget to let associates know how higher headquarters responds to your unit's performance, suggestions, and ideas.

There is another type of outreach that serves a leader well. It involves building and cultivating a large braintrust of talented, high-integrity people. The members of the braintrust serve as advisors, aiding the leader when he faces challenges, large tasks, and ethical issues. My work with the Cable News Network (CNN) has taught me a great deal about how to maximize the value of a braintrust. Judy Milestone, CNN's vice president for guest booking, has established a braintrust of more than 20,000 people who support CNN in many ways. These people help the network to report important news events by sharing their expertise on camera. They assist in helping CNN go to the right places, ask the right questions, and cover both the substance and the nuances of each story. They are people of high integrity who take part in the marvelous service that CNN provides—revealing world news quickly and accurately. Milestone's staff of thirty professionals work very hard to make sure that they identify, schedule, and pre-interview only the very best, up-to-date professionals in their various fields. The credentials of prospective consultants are checked very carefully, and the candidates who seem interested in pushing their own personal agendas are not invited to provide commentary. CNN treats its experts as if they were members of the family. Although the network provides no monetary compensation, it shows appreciation in many ways—thank you calls and letters, invitations to CNN sponsored events, etc. Milestone's exemplary process of carefully selecting and using a braintrust teaches us that a good leader should provide himself or herself with a group of "experts" that will help in times of need and challenge.

My own braintrust is broken into two categories. One is the

general category that includes experts on leadership, planning, ethics, strategy, and military operations. Included in this category are authorities on certain "hot spot" regions of the world—Iraq and Iran; Bosnia, Serbia, and Kosovo; Korea; China; Russia; and Africa. When a crisis develops on the world scene and it appears that military action is imminent, the CEO of CNN or one of his top corporate officers will call me. I immediately exercise my braintrust and send out e-mail messages to several dozen people. I alert them that, within a day or two, I will be going to Atlanta to work full time for CNN. I pose a series of questions and ask for quick answers via e-mail or telephone. Hence, by the time I appear on camera, I have assembled the collective wisdom of a large number of very bright and knowledgeable people.

I also use my braintrust to help me when I am writing my books. When *Rules & Tools for Leaders* was in manuscript form, I sent copies to twenty friends who are especially knowledgeable and experienced in leadership. I asked for and received many comments and criticisms. Using my leadership braintrust, I received more than 1,000 ideas, most of which I have incorporated in this text.

The second category of my braintrust is equally important to me. It is my ethical braintrust. About once a year, I find myself unable to sleep at night, as I worry about an ethical issue that I am facing. So the next morning, I make contact with various members of my ethical braintrust for advice and support. My wife, my two adult children, and about a dozen close friends who have especially high ethical standards provide me with helpful advice as I make my decision.

For example, I recently gave a speech on executive leadership to a large number of senior military officers. One of the officers in the audience—in fact, one of the most senior officers—was clearly drunk. He interrupted my speech twice with noisy, impolite comments. His behavior got even worse after the speech. Since this officer was responsible for the leadership of more than 100,000 military personnel, I felt that he was setting a terrible example. After losing a couple of nights' sleep trying to decide what to do, if anything, about the issue, I turned to my ethical braintrust for advice. I also talked to senior officers, medical doctors, military historians, and people who know the general very well.

After listening to their advice, I decided that I would be remiss if I remained silent on this issue. I took a number of actions. First, I wrote the general and his spouse a supportive letter offering my assistance, telling them that I was praying for them and suggesting that they might seek professional help for the disease of alcoholism. I made a trip to Washington to meet with the top military leader in this general's chain of command, to express my concern and to suggest that he get personally involved before the general made a serious mistake that might cost lives. I also talked at length to a senior military doctor to suggest that he take efforts to assist. Although I did not completely agree with the actions taken (I felt a month in an alcohol rehabilitation program was in order), the general was given very firm counselling, did not get drunk again, and retired quietly about six months later.

Of course, leaders must be careful not to consider building braintrusts and doing outreach their only objectives. There are some leaders who spend so much time consulting with braintrusts on specific issues, doing outreach to other organizations, and serving on outside boards and committees that they spend too little time on the daily needs of their own organizations. These individuals become absentee leaders and, as a result, begin to lose the loyalty and support of the people who work for them. It is the mature leader who keeps outreach and "inreach" in proper balance. As in so many areas of leadership, a good sense of proportion and balance is the key to success.

10
COMPLIMENTING CREATIVELY
saying thank you in many ways

When you first arrive at work, compliment someone; at lunch find another to compliment; before you go home at night be sure to pay a compliment to someone else.

—*Fred Kyler*

A compliment is something like a kiss through a veil.

—*Victor Hugo*

A good leader spends a considerable amount of time complimenting and thanking the people who work for him or her. Indeed, it is quite an art to do this in a way that conveys sincerity, compliments people who should be complimented, and subtly leaves out the few people who do not deserve to be commended.

Casey Kasem, the radio disc jockey, always introduced the Top 40 songs to his listening audience with great enthusiasm. One of the reasons for Kasem's success and popularity was his ability to find *uniqueness* in each song. A combination of his creativity, his commitment to research, and his love for his work made many people want to listen to his show. Years ago, I heard him introduce a song by describing how it was the first time in the history of the Top 40 that a Scottish trio singing a country-western song had made it to the Top 10. His approach triggered a leadership idea. The following week, I made the point to all of my subordinate leaders that they should look for the positive, unusual and special things that their units have been doing. Through careful research and brainstorming, they were able to find things that were unique, were establishing new standards, or were setting new records within their units. In order to express appreciation and recognition, we highlighted these things in the weekly base newspaper, applying descriptive headlines and telling laudatory stories: "Supply Squadron Establishes Record for Servicing F-15's"; "Security Police Set New Record in Processing of Licenses for Automobiles"; "Fighter Squadron and Maintenance Unit Set New Flying Time (or Sortie) Record," etc. This is a marvelous way to make people feel very special; it is a creative way to pay compliments. Many leaders just say, "You all did well," "I'm proud of you," or "Thanks a lot," as though the gratitude was part of a routine. Making the compliment-paying aspect of your leadership more personal and more creative pays dividends in enhancing individual and organizational morale.

The idea of catching people doing things right, rather than catching them doing something wrong, has universal benefit. As a leader, be sensitive to the great advantage of immediate recognition and have compliments, awards, bonuses, and medals at the ready. Thus, when someone does something extraordinary, or something ordinary in an extraordinary way or with extraordinary results, an award is immediately available.

In most organizations, more than 90 percent of the people are working diligently to accomplish the mission, to serve the institution, to make the unit look good, or to make you look good. People generally want to associate with, and participate in, success. It is important to remind yourself often that your people are working hard and doing a fine job. You should spend a lot of time complimenting and thanking them. When you get people together and praise them, there occasionally may be some who do not deserve your praise, but that fact should not deter you from complimenting the group. Those who are not deserving of praise can be dealt with separately and individually. When you thank your associates, do not sound angry. Unfortunately, some leaders try to thank their workers emphatically, but end up sounding like they are chewing the people out. These leaders have not developed the kind of presence that permits them to reach out and figuratively to wrap their arms around their associates, letting them know that they respect and appreciate the work being done. Brilliant, efficient individuals who cannot warmly thank, compliment, and commend their people will always fall significantly short of their full potential as leaders.

In the area of creative compliments, some thought should be given to developing techniques for complimenting individual associates, as well. One of the highest compliments I've ever received was given personally to me by the late General Jerry O'Malley. He explained that the reason he had chosen me to be the Air Force Planner was because the majors and lieutenant colonels in the Plans Directorate had wanted me. By avoiding the conventional rationale that I had some good qualifications for the job and, instead, finding a creative way to compliment me, he really touched me. It was as nice a compliment as I could have imagined, and it meant a lot coming from a man who had a great understanding of people.

Compliments can motivate people to perform at higher levels of excellence and cooperation. This is especially true of the compliments that are well-timed and well-phrased. Conversely, the absence of compliments can be devastating to an organization. Too many leaders take the attitude that their people are "only doing their job" and "that's what they get paid for." The hidden price is low morale and a reduced level of performance.

An important part of thanking and commending people is knowing their names. In very large organizations, it is impossible for leaders to know most of their associates' names, but whenever they are about to present awards, compliment an organization publicly, or give a speech to a significant number of coworkers, they should mention a few names of people in the group who are particularly deserving of praise. In such situations, leaders must do some homework and, if possible, meet briefly ahead of time with those individuals who are going to be singled out publicly. If you are in this position, ask lots of questions prior to the ceremony or speech. Find out if the organization has received any outside recognition lately, and if anyone in the audience has done anything particularly noteworthy recently (such as saving someone's life, recovering from major surgery, getting married, having a baby, returning after a long absence, being elected to an important position). Note any sports events, such as a softball, golf, tennis, or bowling tournaments, that the organization recently has won.

Since many associates also value praise from their peers and from their subordinates, you should look for ways to feed compliments back through the organization. Whenever an associate tells me about how a colleague has done a fine job, I say, "Thanks for telling me; I'll thank him [or her] personally—but I would ask you to pass on that praise to him [or her] yourself, too."

Usually, short handwritten notes are greatly appreciated: "I have been thinking about your suggestion at the last staff meeting and I think it is superb. I plan to take action on it soon."; "Many thanks."; "Congratulations on your birthday. Your contributions over the past year have been first rate. I hope you enjoy working here as much as we enjoy having you as part of our corporate family."; "It is a great privilege for me to share ideas with and learn from you."

Also, if possible, take individuals whom you would like to thank out to lunch, hold a workshop with them to get their ideas, or, in general, spend some time with them. During this time, call them by their first names. You can "pair" or "bond" with individuals at lower levels in the organization by using these techniques. As they return to their workplaces, the associates will spread the word that you are approachable, know their names, and show interest in their ideas. Trust and loyalty will grow throughout the organization. And don't forget that if you know your associates' hopes and dreams, if you understand and empathize with their hardships and complaints, you can better thank and compliment them. Moreover, you can better plan and make decisions for the good of the organization and the people that you serve. (For further guidance on how to thank your associates, see Appendix A, Checklist #15.)

Finally, a leader also must know how to *accept* compliments. An excellent rule of thumb is to pass on every compliment that you receive to your associates. After all, in almost every case, the success was theirs—their ideas, their efficiency, their hard work, and their creativity, all in marvelous combinations. Praising creatively should be at the top of the list when it comes to a leader's communication skills. And you'll get better at it with practice. Follow the advice of Letitia Baldridge: "Learn how to pay compliments. Start with members of your family, and you will find it will become easier later in life to compliment others. It's a great asset."

11
HIRING
the right people for the right jobs

Recipe for success: First, make a reputation for creative genius. Second, surround yourself with partners who are better than you are. Third, leave them to get on with it.
— *David Ogilvey*

Mistrust a subordinate who never finds fault with his superior.
— *John C. Collins*

As a leader, one of your most important responsibilities is the recruitment and selection of immediate subordinates and other key people in the organization. Personnel records and resumes are useful starting points in identifying those individuals who are clearly strong candidates for the position under consideration. However, additional research needs to be done. Contacting individuals who know the candidate can be a very enlightening process. It is particularly useful to talk to people who have been the individual's supervisors in recent years, in order to get candid evaluations of the candidate's performance in other job situations. This task requires a considerable amount of time. However, all of the research is worth the time it takes, for it ensures that the selection process is as complete and objective as possible. Still, in many cases, research alone is not enough and an interview is necessary.

The interview should be conducted systematically. I strongly suggest that you use a checklist. (See Appendix A, Checklist #3.) However, the checklist should be in your head rather than on paper, in order to increase the informality of the interview process. Below are several key questions to ask during the interview.

Do you want this job and why? This should be the first question asked of a prospective key associate. If the candidate is not really interested in the job, has serious reservations, or has motivations that you do not find useful or particularly attractive, the interview can be wrapped up quickly and the individual eliminated from consideration. If you are satisfied and impressed by the response, continue the interview.

Why should I hire you? What are your strengths and what are your weaknesses? These questions sometimes set an interviewee back a bit, but they are very useful to find out how introspective the individual is. If the candidate lists a large number of strengths and no weaknesses, or vice versa, you may have identified an individual who will not serve you well. Someone who not only outlines individual strengths but also is aware of and working on weaknesses is an individual who probably deserves very serious consideration. On the other hand, neither a candidate who is arrogantly self-assured, nor one who lacks fundamental self-confidence, is likely to be a major contributor to your organization.

What are the best books and professional journals that you have read in recent years? Why do you consider them so good? What insights did you gain from these readings? Find out how well-read the candidate is—how intellectually curious; how open to the ideas, suggestions, and insights that good books can provide; how well this person is keeping up with his or her discipline or profession. It has been my experience that people who are not widely read and who do not have the interest to read professional journals and books that help them improve are basically self-limited. They are not likely to grow and to make major contributions beyond the level of their present competence. If you find a person who is well-read, you probably can gain some stimulating and useful insights and have a discussion that will be a learning experience on both sides. Often, the best leaders are the ones who are intellectually curious.

What is your leadership philosophy and style? If I were to ask your present associates how they would describe your leadership style, what would they say? This is a good way to ascertain whether the individual knows how to operate efficiently, knows what subordinates feel, knows how to set goals and priorities, and knows how to be introspective. The answers quickly can draw out the attitude that the individual has toward subordinates and their possible discomfort with his or her personal style. The candidate's response, in combination with what you find out from other sources, can give you an understanding of how well this individual grasps the realities of his or her present situation.

If you are not selected for this position, who would you recommend? Such a question will reveal how the person judges the job and the qualities that are needed for it, and how closely the applicant is in contact with other individuals with similar qualifications. It also will bring out how willing the individual is to acknowledge that there may be others who are as qualified—or better qualified—for the job.

Are there any "skeletons in your closet"? This is a sensitive question and is best asked in a more considerate way, such as, "Are there any general health, family, psychiatric, or other problems that are worrying you because they may cause you difficulties or prevent your full effectiveness in this job?" or "Is there anything that would be helpful for me to know now which might be an embarrassment if it surfaces later?" In any case, such a question needs to be asked to help determine how candid the individual is willing to be. You may want to hire the person regardless of his or her response, but it's useful to have all of the cards on the table. If important information is withheld from you and you find it out through other sources, you will discover that this person is unwilling to be completely candid with you.

What are your long-term personal goals? It's helpful to find out where an individual is heading in life. Does this person want to work for you forever or does he or she just want this job for a year or two? What are his or her goals after this? Is this applicant hyperambitious or ambitious in a positive way? From the answers to these questions, you can gain a wider understanding of the candidate's goals and potential.

If you were in charge of this organization, what would you do? (Of course, this question is most appropriate for candidates who know the organization quite well.) By asking the interviewee to wear figuratively the leader's shoes, you will be able to detect if he or she has original ideas and insights, as well as a willingness to speak up about aspects of the organization that he or she finds inadequate or uncomfortable. If, for instance, the candidate says nothing, you might want to ask yourself, "Does this person have the ability to make significant changes where needed, or is this someone who will always be satisfied with the status quo?"

What is it that annoys you in your present organization? This is a good question to ask someone who already works for you, as well as a valuable question to ask a potential employee, regarding his or her present organization. You can learn a great deal about a candidate's personality through the response. Also, an interviewee may reveal aspects about his or her interaction in an organizational framework that may reinforce your desire to hire the person, or, conversely, give you indications that you would not be comfortable with this individual.

What are the standards of integrity in your present organization? Use this question to lead into the integrity question. Does the prospective employee have high standards of personal integrity? Does he or she set high standards of institutional integrity? Does the interviewee think or care much about integrity? This can lead to a useful discussion on the issues of institutional and personal ethics and the role that they play in an organizational framework.

Whom in your present organization do you respect the most and why? This question tends to highlight certain aspects of personality and background that may provide insights into what a candidate thinks are the important aspects of leadership. If a person admires a strong leader and knows why, if that individual knows what leadership qualities he or she would like to emulate, you may have discovered an individual who seriously has been thinking about leadership and who may be the kind of person who you would want to hire as one of your subordinate leaders.

What is the toughest problem you have faced in your career? How did you handle it? These questions can be a useful way to determine how well the individual has been tested and what he or she has learned from a difficult experience. It is one way to determine how introspective an individual is. Also, you can gather an idea about how the candidate deals with failure, and whether he or she can function under pressure.

How would you handle a sexual harassment problem? This question and the follow-up questions should draw out a number of insights. Has the individual had any experience with sexual harassment cases? How sensitive is the individual to the issue and how much training has been received? How strongly does the candidate feel about the issue?

What values do you hold dear and why? An interviewee's answer to this rather personal question should give you a feeling for how deeply he or she has thought about the subject. Answers involving high integrity, character, concern for others, altruism, and service above self will tell you one thing. Answers that discuss job fulfillment or opportunities for promotion will tell you something else. Here is an area where your follow-up questions may give you a profoundly helpful understanding of what drives the interviewee.

Since the hiring of immediate subordinates is important, it should be delegated only in certain situations. If you, as the boss, have a trusted deputy who has great insights into the personalities of individuals, has had a lot of experience with interviewing people, has a good feeling for the organization, and knows your particular desires and proclivities, delegating the

hiring practice to him or her makes good sense. Also, it is sometimes useful to draw together a search committee that may have
expertise that you don't have, and whose members would be
capable of asking the most relevant questions. You can use this
committee to screen out and reduce the list to a small number,
but, ultimately, the leader has the responsibility to make the
choice.

You should be involved actively in hiring those individuals
who work directly for you. Correspondingly, under normal
conditions, subordinate leaders should be given the authority to
hire *their* subordinates. If a big leader wishes to maintain veto
authority over the hiring of key subordinates whom he or she
will not supervise directly, this veto should be used with great
care. It can help reduce cronyism on the part of subordinate
leaders, but it actually should be used very seldom.

Finally, when evaluating various candidates for a key position, fully consider the subtle but important aspect commonly
known as "chemistry." The chemistry factor is critical not only
to subordinate-leader interactions, but also to peer relationships
among subordinate associates. This is one of the reasons that
interviews are important; a set of personnel records cannot help
very much in determining how well an individual will fit into
the environment that you have established in your organization.
But one caution about chemistry is in order: in seeking associates with the right chemistry, there is always the danger that
prejudices and biases of which you may not even be aware will
sway a decision. Be careful not to use "bad chemistry" as an
excuse for not hiring a well-qualified candidate who is not of the
same race or sex, or who does not come from the same cultural,
social, or educational background as you. The top personnel
officer also must avoid narrowing the candidates down in order
to satisfy the leader's hidden (or not-so-hidden) prejudices.

12

COUNSELLING ASSOCIATES

the value of one-on-ones

Encourage your staff to be candid with you. Ask their advice and listen to it. Top bananas have no monopoly on ideas.
                                    —David Ogilvey

Many receive advice, only the wise profit from it.
                                    —Syrus

About once every six months, a leader of an organization should have private sessions with the associates who work directly under him or her, to deal specifically with performance counselling. The purpose of these sessions is to trade thoughts, insights, and suggestions, and to learn about the health of the organization. It is an opportunity for personal counselling, but, to an even greater extent, it is an opportunity for associates to talk quietly, off the record, with the boss in a meaningful way, to get things off their chests and to suggest ideas and initiatives. Furthermore, individual objectives for improvement can be set for review six months later. These private meetings also give associates the feeling that their input really counts and that the boss is truly interested in listening to their ideas and criticisms.

Most good leaders look forward to counselling their associates because it is a time for praise and encouragement. Associates should also look forward to these sessions, for they can provide a marvelous opportunity to get the full attention of the boss on important personal and institutional issues. In observing leaders from many nations at various levels, it has been my experience that these one-on-one sessions are the exception, rather than the rule. Although leaders talk about how they counsel their people, in actuality, counselling sessions seldom take place. A quick gathering in the hall, a brief comment or two at a staff meeting, or a passing remark here and there are not counselling sessions. Important issues should be discussed in prearranged, private meetings at which the following (or similar) questions are asked.

What aspects of this organization do you like the most? It is useful to start the session on a positive note. This question can be an "icebreaker" since the associate may be a bit uncomfortable during the first few minutes in the front office with the boss.

What issues concern you most? This question allows the associate to voice those areas of real heartburn. It might be that the associate does not like the job, the work hours, the level of authority, the living conditions, the pay, or the amount of recognition received. It is a good opportunity to "smoke out" those things that really bother your employee.

What are your ideas for improving this organization? As a leader, you are in charge not only of gathering ideas, but also of finding out where the "idea people" are. In every organization, there are some people who have especially useful and innovative ideas. This question often helps identify the folks who are deeply committed to improving the organization and who have talents to make things happen.

Of what policies, procedures, tactics, subordinate organizations, systems, etc., should we divest ourselves and on what kind of schedule (now, next year, five years from now, etc.)? Here's a way to discover whether the individual has thought about the problems of the organization—what programs should be abandoned, what things are inhibiting the accomplishment of the organization's mission. The associate now has the chance to explain what approaches were useful in the past but are no longer useful and the opportunity to offer his or her own ideas for both divestiture candidates and for a divestiture strategy.

In your judgment, who are the most innovative, helpful, and cooperative people in this organization? "Who are the people who are not pulling their load?" is often an unfair question and one that people are reluctant to answer. So instead, ask your associate to identify the *best* coworkers. You'll not only find out who the valuable employees are, but you'll also notice, over time, who is seldom or never mentioned. The ones who are not mentioned are normally the ones who are not pulling their load, not being cooperative, or who have some other problem. In most cases, you already will know who the best employees are, but, on occasion, you will be surprised. Someone who is particularly quiet, for example, might be highlighted as an absolutely marvelous and contributing individual.

What are your personal goals while you are in this organization? This is a fine way to ascertain the dreams and aspirations of your associates. Some will prefer to stay at their present levels; others will want to move to another division or location; still others will want to move upward. Answers to this question can be very helpful when you conduct personnel planning. Here you get an idea of an employee's long-range plans: "Where (to what job) would you like to go next?"; "Why?"; "When would you like to go?"; "What ambitions do you have?"; "How happy are you here?" Furthermore, you can help an associate who does not have specific goals to develop them, as well as a schedule for when those goals should be accomplished.

What do you consider to be your most significant weaknesses? If the individual doesn't think any weaknesses exist, you may have a problem right there. As often happens, the individual may outline personal weaknesses fairly well, but might miss one or two areas. This gives you the opportunity to probe gently about a person's ability to write, to speak, to cooperate, to lead, to manage. You can also probe into other areas of possible weakness that may not have been identified. Although a delicate question, it often opens the door to excellent counselling opportunities.

What do you think your chances are for promotion to the next level, and in what time frame? This line of questioning gives you an opportunity to have individuals evaluate their own potential for moving up to higher levels of responsibility. You will find out whether their expectations are inflated, as they are in some cases. If they do have inflated expectations and you are aware of weak or mediocre professional records, you can give them a candid appraisal. It is important that you be frank, as well as factual, so that individuals with poor performance records are not destroyed emotionally if they fail to be promoted at some later date.

What bothers you the most about my decisions and my leadership style? In what areas have my decisions or policies caused you to waste your time? Here's a great opportunity to find out a little bit about yourself. Answers to the question may include: "You're too intense."; "You don't listen well."; "You interrupt often."; "You're too hard on people."; "You've put too much emphasis in certain areas and not enough in others."; "What we are doing in a certain area is a waste of time and money." Some people, of course, will tell you that you're wonderful and not give you any indication of your problem areas, but the better, more mature subordinates almost always will say, "Yes, there are a few areas; let me make a few suggestions."

What are the goals that you have established for your organization? Here you are asking subordinates what goals they have set for their specific organizations. Do their goals conform to the ones you have established for the parent organization? Perhaps the individual has established goals that are more thoughtful or innovative than your own.

Please evaluate the performance of the organization, unit, or group that you led over the past six months. Please outline the high and low points of the period. This is a useful way to ascertain the objectivity of subordinate leaders when it comes to their own organizations. You can also get an idea of how willing they are to take responsibility for setbacks, as well as to whom/what they attribute any impressive successes.

What self-improvement programs do you have underway? More specifically, "Are you pursuing advanced education?"; "Are you taking professional courses?"; "Are you in a Toastmaster's Club to learn how to be a better speaker?"; "Are you taking a speed-reading course?" If the individual is doing nothing for self-development, you have an opportunity to highlight the value of self-improvement.

What is your approach to personal and family wellness and to community involvement? You can learn how the associate finds relaxation, how effective his or her wellness goals are for personal and family time, as well as for time with coworkers, and how committed he or she is to supporting important community activities. Simply by raising this question, you may help the individual give serious consideration to these issues.

A counselling checklist is provided in Appendix A of this book (Checklist #7). The checklist should not be read; it should be in your head. At the end of the counselling session, you have the responsibility not only to point out the strengths of the individual, but also to point out his or her weaknesses. If you do not alert your associates when they are not doing particularly well, you are not conducting honest, fair, and complete counselling. This endeavor takes a lot of time and is hard work. Sometimes the associate's reaction to criticism is very emotional, but counselling is something that needs to be scheduled regularly and done well. For each one-on-one session, you should allow one hour. Often the session may last only twenty or thirty minutes, but there is a chance that serious issues will surface and require you to listen for a long time. As a general rule, the session should start and end on positive notes. Even if the individual has not been performing well, a compliment at the end of the session is important.

Sometimes, your counselling session with a subordinate must concentrate wholly on his or her shortcomings or failures. It is both tempting and easy to avoid or postpone these sessions, but they must be done in a timely and tactful manner. If an employee makes a serious mistake that clearly requires corrective action, immediately call a private meeting. Public admonishment should be avoided, but private counselling should take place quickly and firmly, and all important areas should be covered carefully and systematically. An excellent example of this type of counselling was Robert E. Lee's session with J.E.B. Stuart, when Stuart arrived at the Gettysburg battlefield two days late. The following passage comes from my favorite book, Michael Shaara's Pulitzer Prize-winning historical novel, *The Killer Angels:*

> He saw a man coming toward him, easy gait, rolling and serene, instantly recognizable: Jeb Stuart. Lee stood up. This must be done. Stuart came up, saluted pleasantly, took off the plumed hat and bowed.
>
> 'You wish to see me, sir?'
>
> 'I asked to see you alone,' Lee said quietly. 'I wished to speak with you alone, away from other officers. That has not been possible until now. I am sorry to keep you up so late.'
>
> 'Sir, I was not asleep,' Stuart drawled, smiled, gave the sunny impression that sleep held no importance, none at all.
>
> Lee thought: here's one with faith in himself. Must protect that. And yet, there's a lesson to be learned. He said, 'Are you aware, General, that there are officers on my staff who have requested your court-martial?'
>
> Stuart froze. His mouth hung open. He shook his head once quickly, then cocked it to one side.
>
> Lee said, 'I have not concurred. But it is the opinion of some excellent officers that you have let us all down.'
>
> 'General Lee,' Stuart was struggling. Lee thought: now there will be anger. 'Sir,' Stuart said tightly, 'if you will tell me who these gentlemen . . .'
>
> 'There will be none of that.' Lee's voice was cold and sharp. He spoke as you speak to a child, a small child, from a great height. 'There is no time for that.'
>
> 'I only ask that I be allowed—'
>
> Lee cut him off. 'There is no time,' Lee said. He was not a man to speak this way to a brother officer, a fellow Virginian; he shocked Stuart to silence with the iciness of his voice. Stuart stood like a

beggar, his hat in his hands.

'General Stuart,' Lee said slowly, 'you were the eyes of this army.' He paused.

Stuart said softly, a pathetic voice, 'General Lee, if you please . . .' But Lee went on.

'You were my eyes. Your mission was to screen this army from the enemy cavalry and to report any movement by the enemy's main body. That mission was not fulfilled.'

Stuart stood motionless.

Lee said, 'You left this army without word of your movements, or of the movements of the enemy, for several days. We were forced into battle without adequate knowledge of the enemy's position, or strength, without knowledge of the ground. It is only by God's grace that we have escaped disaster.'

'General Lee.' Stuart was in pain, and the old man felt pity, but this was necessary; it had to be done as a bad tooth has to be pulled, and there was no turning away. Yet even now he felt the pity rise, and he wanted to say, it's all right, boy, it's all right; this is only a lesson, just one painful quick moment of learning, over in a moment, hold on, it'll be all right. His voice began to soften. He could not help it.

'It is possible that you misunderstood my orders. It is possible that I did not make myself clear. Yet this must be clear; you with your cavalry are the eyes of the army. Without your cavalry, we are blind, and that has happened once, but must never happen again.'

There was a full moment of silence. It was done. Lee wanted to reassure him, but he waited, giving it time to sink in, to take effect, like medicine. Stuart stood breathing audibly. After a moment he reached down and unbuckled his sword, theatrically, and handed it over with high drama in his face. Lee grimaced, annoyed, put his hands behind his back, half turned his face. Stuart was saying that since he no longer held the General's trust, but Lee interrupted with acid vigor.

'I have told you that there is no time for that. There is a fight tomorrow, and we need you. We need every man, God knows. You must take what I have told you and learn from it as a man does. There has been a mistake. It will not happen again. I know your quality. You are a good soldier. You are as good a cavalry officer as I have known, and your service to this army has been invaluable. I have learned to rely on your information; all your reports are always accurate. But no report is useful if it does not reach us. And that is what I wanted you to know. Now.' He lifted a hand. 'Let us talk no more of this.'

Regular counselling has enormous value to a leader. I cannot emphasize too strongly how much I have gained from the constructive criticism, new perspectives, and fresh ideas that these sessions yield. They are well worth the time of all executives and associates.

An excellent way to transition new associates into a regular counselling system and to gain many insights was suggested to me by Air Force General John Barry: "On the original meeting with new folks entering the organization, I give each one a homework assignment. I tell them that they have a great advantage over the rest of us, for they are looking at things for the first time. I instruct them to send me an 'eyes only' memo within two weeks, telling me the things they like and dislike about the organization, its facilities, the heroes/heroines who may have helped them, etc." Such a practice allows the new-comers to feel that their opinions count from the beginning, and also widens your perspective of the organization.

13
TEACHING AND READING
leadership essentials

To teach is to learn twice.
> *—Joseph Jaubert*

If you think education is expensive—try ignorance.
> *—Derek Bok*

Good leaders tend to be good teachers who use various means to exercise "teachership" responsibility. Staff meetings, for instance, are marvelous teaching opportunities, as are welcoming briefings for new people in the organization, speaking engagements at professional schools, and, of course, teaching in one-on-one situations.

General Fox Conner, the great teacher of Eisenhower, Marshall, and others, serves as a wonderful role model. His teachership was quiet and subtle. He looked for no praise, but received great satisfaction from the brilliant performance of his students as they led the U.S. Army in World War II and in the post-war era. Conner's teachership success illustrates that a great leader, in guiding subordinate leaders, also teaches them how to be leaders themselves. By setting an example for others to emulate, by taking the time to teach, and by teaching systematically and regularly, such a leader can greatly affect the present and the future.

Part of teachership is planting good ideas in the minds of associates in such subtle ways that they soon feel these ideas are their own. A good leader probably has a lot of good ideas, but he or she will be a more effective leader if new ideas are perceived as and credited with having come from others within the organization. If associates feel that the organization has reached high levels of excellence on its own, the leader has been very successful indeed. Leaders should take silent satisfaction when their ideas are captured by others. It is a wise leader who takes the attitude of first grade teachers, who, at the end of the year, receive no thanks from the children, but know they have prepared them well for the next level.

One useful teaching opportunity is to make a short, punchy videotape. Start by introducing yourself; then discuss the history, philosophy, goals, and priorities of the organization. Speak about the importance of the mission and the important role that *all* associates play. This tape will have many uses, as it can be shown to new employees, visitors, customers, and members of the media. If resources permit, the videotape should be done professionally. Such a tape is most effective when it is short—ten to fifteen minutes—and when it is updated every year or two.

Periodic off-site retreats are excellent teaching opportunities. I have found the following guidelines especially conducive to enhancing communication, creativity, and teamwork. Every year, you should invite your key associates to a two- or three-day retreat. Before going on the retreat, it is useful to send a short questionnaire to all the people who will be attending. The questionnaire should inquire about the high and low points of the year; the new initiatives that the associates would like to take next year; who a good guest speaker for the retreat would be; and suggested topics of discussion for the retreat.

The retreat should be held in a relaxed atmosphere, in a location that is geographically removed from the normal work area. Attendees should remain at the site overnight. Sports should be scheduled in the late afternoons; round robin tennis tournaments, and volleyball and softball games work well as sports mixers. Roommates should be paired so that each new associate rooms with a person who has been with the organization for some time.

Open your retreat with a general statement on the organization's philosophy, goals, priorities, and concerns, and review the past year by highlighting both the ups and downs. A "fever" chart, showing highs and lows, can be helpful in this regard. Then, establish the rules for the retreat—for example, all discussions are off the record and everyone should speak with total candor. You should ask questions and encourage questions: "What successes have we enjoyed and what have been the secrets to these successes?"; "What is really bothering you about the organization and my leadership style?"; "What opportunities are we missing?"; "What mistakes have we made or are we making?"; "How can we make next year even more productive?"; "How am I wasting your time?" Next, emphasize the major upcoming events and explain why they are important to the organization. It is important to thank associates for their outstanding work and encourage them to seek even higher levels of excellence next year.

Another good way to exercise teachership is to establish and maintain a reading program. It is often said that the really tough jobs cause people to burn up intellectual capital because these individuals stay so busy that they have little time to read, research, or reflect. Leaders who manage their time well can continue to read and gain insights from the best books and articles related to their fields. Leaders should read good histories, biographies, and autobiographies, as well as books on management, leadership, strategy, planning, and the long-term future. (See Appendix E for a short list of the better works on leadership.) Consequently, one of the subjects that should be addressed periodically is a discussion of the best books that you and your associates have read over the past year. You should have cerebral energy and should demonstrate that energy not only by establishing a systematic reading program for yourself, but also by encouraging associates to read valuable material. Display recently read books in prominent places in your office—on the office coffee table, for example. As you read new books, previous ones should be replaced. In this way, you can demonstrate to all of your associates and visitors your commitment to a serious reading program. When you read a particularly outstanding book, buy a number of copies and give them to key associates. In addition, establish a system that ensures that the better professional journals circulate throughout the organization.

One way for you to maximize the value of a reading program is to make comments in the margins of each book, engaging the author in a running conversation. This practice tracks your thoughts and often generates some unexpected ideas and answers. Another technique is to mark the book with a "quote-file" notation. Then the secretary can place a specific quote in a file, and you can use this material in speeches, articles, and letters. In this way, you can ensure that future speeches have lots of fresh material which has been obtained through the reading program. A wonderful way to establish and maintain a productive reading program is to read, on a weekly basis, a significant number of book reviews. Most professional journals have book review sections. *The New York Times'* Sunday edition also includes first-rate book reviews. Generally, it is a good idea not to buy a book until you have read at least two book reviews that confirm that reading the book is worth your valuable time.

If you read two books each month, you are doing a good job of maintaining cerebral energy and intellectual curiosity. I suggest that you mix serious books of nonfiction that relate directly or indirectly to your chosen field with "fun" books of fiction, biography, humor, travel, etc. To further maximize the value of reading time, you may want to read the first and last chapter of each book. If, after reading the first and last chapters, you have not been inspired sufficiently by the author's ideas and insights, reading the rest of the book is likely to be a waste of your time.

When you go home for the weekend, try to avoid taking the in-box home. If you manage your time well, you should get to the bottom of the in-box by the end of the week and have time for outside reading on weekends, as well as on holidays and trips. And if you are one of those top executives who wakes up very early, think about using that extra time to read before you come to work. In addition to benefiting yourself, you will be giving your staff a chance to clean up the work of the previous day and to get ready for their queries and demands. A wonderful way to break a lifelong habit of coming to work early is to schedule morning reading time at home.

Since leaders should be visionaries and planners, they should spend some time reading books about the long-term future. There are a number of excellent mind-stretching books that can help leaders ask their strategic planners the right questions. The following is a short list of books in this category: Don Tapscott's *The Digital Economy*; Hamish McRae's *The World in 2020;* and Michael Moynihan's *The Coming American Renaissance.*

If a leader has been a good reader, thinker, and teacher, the organization will be in stronger shape, and the job for the next leader will be easier. If a leader is spending a great deal of time teaching, and only a modest amount of time problem solving, he or she probably has the priorities straight.

14

CREATING A STRATEGIC VISION

the role of planning

*The basis of individual and national progress is the willingness
to sacrifice the present for the future. That is the way nations
get ahead and that is the way individuals get ahead.*

—William Feather

Where there is no vision, the people perish.

—Proverbs XXIX, 18

The great leaders of our time have been not only effective opera-
tors and decision-makers, but also people of vision. They have
had marvelous insight into what is possible, how to set and articulate goals, and how to motivate their people to strive successfully for these goals. Great leaders are usually great planners.

Having served in a number of key planning positions in
government and having written two books on strategic planning, I have learned that many leaders do not understand how
to accomplish systematic planning. One of the major problems
is that individuals within organizations often view planning
from very different perspectives. Senior executives must understand that planning in the budget office is quite different from
planning in the operational divisions, or from planning in the
personnel or marketing directorates. It is the task of the leader
to establish a system that allows specialized planning to take
place, but always within the context of a cohesive strategic planning system.

There are several important rules regarding the relationship between the top leaders and the planning staff at the cor-

porate, agency, or service headquarters. First, the top leaders must have direct access to the planners and should schedule meetings with them on a regular basis. They must read, know, and understand the organization's most significant plans. Lastly, the top leaders must discipline themselves so that key decisions support the strategic plan.

All organizations should prepare a strategic plan and update it annually. The strategic plan should be brief, usually about ten to twelve pages. It should be signed by the top leader and should be distributed widely throughout the organization, though it may require a classified supplement to ensure that competitors and others do not have full access to sensitive technologies, concepts, or impending decisions. Over the course of the year, this plan should be referred to periodically. Calling it "our strategic plan" is a useful technique in getting support throughout the organization. Key associates should be assured that the leader will make decisions based on the outlined vision. If an organization has a strategic vision that includes specific goals and priorities, daily decision-making is much more likely to have real coherence. Goals charge people up; they ignite the human spirit. If goals are constructed carefully and are well-understood, if they enhance the success of the mission, both good and bad luck can be better managed.

It is important to recognize the symbolic value of a strategic plan. Even if you do not wish to take any major initiatives in the near term, many employees want, need, and expect some kind of strategic vision for their organization. A strategic plan provides a clear path that the associates can follow.

Another important element of planning is divestiture planning. All large organizations need to pursue aggressively divestiture strategies to ensure that they do not retain outdated or antiquated policies, offices, doctrines, or research and development programs. Economic analysis in a profit-making firm normally points to areas of weakness and obsolescence within the organization. In government, divestiture is a more difficult process because outmoded areas are harder to identify and more difficult to exorcise from the organization. The strategic planners can help in this regard by laying out an overall structure for the organization that reaches ten to twenty years into the future. This helps you to focus attention on areas that will not be relevant by the year 2015, 2020, 2025, etc. By working in close coordination with strategic planners and a divestiture team, the top leaders can develop a scheme for phasing out those elements that should not be present two decades hence. One of the great problem areas that most top leaders face is a reluctance to plan for a period beyond the leader's expected tenure. This is an acute problem in federal and state government, where many leaders expect to retain their positions for no more than four years. These restricted time horizons are a serious detriment to a strategic planning process.

Divestiture ideally should take place before obsolescence sets in, thus before the organization, system, or doctrine is in decline. Preemptive divestiture should be the goal so that buggy whips, typewriters, and "horse cavalries" of the future are phased out much more promptly than they were in the past. The top leader must carefully protect divestiture teams. Many field and staff officials resent individuals who recommend initiatives for divestiture, since they usually mean the loss of jobs, power, and prestige.

When changes in power and positions are necessary, you should adhere to the "dignified burial" guideline and spend a considerable portion of your time and energy helping the employees find new and exciting opportunities in the firm, if at all possible. Other employees will be watching how you manage the divestiture process. If you accomplish it ruthlessly and with little consideration for their fellow workers who are affected, this action will have a negative impact on the morale of the entire organization.

A good example of creative divestiture was shared with me by a CEO of a large newspaper chain. Because of the very rapidly changing technological situation in the publishing business, he decided to form a small software team to design a better system to get reporters' stories into print. The team came up with a very innovative way to use and intranet personal computers. The system not only saved a lot of time and money, but also was very popular with the reporters. A number of other newspapers and publishing firms learned of this new system and started to buy the software packages that his team had designed. For a brief period of time, the publisher considered going into the software business, but then decided that he wanted to stay true to his strategic plan of remaining within the boundaries of a communications company. Hence, he sold off his software business at a considerable profit.

One of my most rewarding experiences as a teacher of strategic thinking and planning occurred during the late 1990s. The top leaders at Texas Instruments in Dallas asked John Warden and me to teach them military strategy. Warden, an Air Force Colonel when he was the architect of the air campaign in the Gulf War of 1991, is the wisest person that I know in the area of strategic thinking and planning. The Texas Instruments executives seemed fascinated with a number of military concepts: the indirect attack; the principle of mass; the use of reserve forces; making winning the peace a more important strategic goal than winning the war; keeping a strategic focus; and techniques of combat leadership. Soon after our workshops, Texas Instruments decided to take a very aggressive approach to divestiture, in order to focus more attention on digital signal processing—a technology that has a very bright future. Texas Instruments' decision to sell off its defense business and its notebook computer business has turned out to be a classic example of brilliant strategic action and divestiture.

No matter what business a company is in, it is often useful for leaders to ask themselves periodically if the company is staying within the context of what it knows how to do. When a company wanders too far from its field of expertise, it often gets into serious trouble. Successful CEOs should avoid the tendency to assume that just because they can run a firm well, they can run anything well. Technical competence in the company's major endeavors is an important attribute for the top leader. If he or she doesn't have it, the likelihood of failure increases. Hence, divestiture is not just unloading the "dogs," it is also selling off the parts of the business that do not fit within the corporate "essence." There are similar situations in government and the military. For example, General Marshall was very wise to support an autonomous, separate U.S. Air Force so the Army in the post-World War II period could concentrate on its strength—ground combat.

As a new leader takes over a large organization, two of the most important questions are: "What is the strategic plan?" and "Who are the strategic planners?" If a leader of a large organization is not committed to an institutionalized planning process, he or she is likely to become merely a caretaker who is unable to raise the organization to higher levels of performance. Leaders should remember Lincoln's insight, "A mind stretched by a new idea never returns to its original dimension." Strategic planners can and should stretch the mind of the leader, and they should do so regularly. The strategic planning division that has direct access to both the chief executive officer and the other top officials within corporate headquarters and the field agencies can be both a marvelous clearinghouse and an effective conduit for ideas and innovations.

A major goal of a planning system is to encourage creativity and innovation throughout the organization. Many leaders give lip service to innovation, while failing to create either the climate or the organizational structure to encourage it. Periodically, leaders should examine the quality, quantity, and velocity of innovation within their organizations. They should be open to new ideas while being sensitive to the turbulence that the implementation of new ideas can often cause.

The velocity of innovation has two components: the speed and ease by which new ideas can reach the top-level leaders, and the speed and ease of decision and the implementation processes. Leaders should measure these two aspects from time to time; auditors and inspection teams can assist in this assessment. Leaders should look for ways to increase the velocity of innovation. Too many leaders tolerate organizational structures that make the movement of new ideas from originator to key decision-makers both slow and difficult. Many large organizations are like a long corridor with dozens of doors. If any of the doors is locked, the idea dies. Leaders must not only reduce the number of doors; they must also ensure that many people have keys to the ones that remain.

The Model Installation Program of the Department of Defense provides a useful example of both innovation and organizational autonomy that is worth examining. The program gives the post or base commanders the opportunity to make decisions on their own, in order to operate more efficiently and effectively. They are able to keep the money they save and use it largely as they choose, to improve the site's operation. In the past, such savings were returned to the Federal Treasury. This former arrangement provided little incentive for base or post officials to seek improvements actively. The Model Installation Program has many more people looking for efficiencies so that funds for badly needed improvements can be generated. The substance and velocity of innovation has improved decidedly as a result of this imaginative DOD program.

Part of the planning process is taking a long-range view of the organizational structure. This will ensure that as goals, priorities, technology, and the workforce change, the organization will adjust to meet the new opportunities and challenges. There is a tendency for executives to err in one of two directions. On the one side, some leaders and institutions love to reorganize and do so too often. This causes unnecessary disruption and turbulence within their organizations and, at times, within neighboring and supporting organizations. My best example in this regard is the U.S. Army. The turbulence that results from constant restructuring not only hurts the Army, but confuses the other military services that must work with and support the Army. Leaders who have a tendency to reorganize often should heed the words of Norm Augustine, who wrote, "Remember: New Tree, Same Monkeys."

The error of the other side of the spectrum is more common: the failure of leaders to anticipate the need for organizational change as they carry out their various plans. A close friend who is a CEO of a large, private corporation aggressively acquired a number of companies within a four-year period. He soon found himself in a situation in which his president had seventeen general managers reporting to him (as opposed to only eight managers, four years prior). After a frantic year of impossibly long days, the CEO reorganized and placed a number of the smaller units of his expanded company under a district manager. The president's span of control was significantly decreased and the company flourished. Leaders who are good planners will make reorganization part of their acquisition strategy, so as they acquire more companies (or, conversely, divest themselves of companies), the organization will be ready to handle the new realities.

The strategic planning done by some of the pharmaceutical and biotechnology companies, as they identified major medical needs (anti-cholesterol drugs, blood-clot destroyers, etc.), offers a fine example of well-placed strategy. These companies committed significant research and development resources to cutting-edge projects, and consequently developed drugs of major health-saving and economic importance. The dramatic success that can result from good planning is evident.

All planning systems have the potential to become too rigid and out of touch with reality. However, if you create a vision based on careful thought and research, you can lead the organization to new heights of performance and effectiveness. Conversely, you will miss opportunities if you, for ideological (or any other) reasons, reject planning. A combination of good systematic planning and flexible "ad-hocracy" can lead to extraordinary results.

As you communicate with your associates in meetings, through speeches, and through newsletters and newspapers, you can help your organization keep a commitment to strategic planning. To use my favorite phrase in this regard, "I am interested in the future because that's where I plan to spend the rest of my life."

15

PERSONALITY AND HEALTH TESTING

tools for the enlightened leader

The first trait that is common among those who are assured a place in history is that of being predisposed to continual self-improvement. Those who have it are dynamically regenerative.

—*James Stockdale*

O wad some Power the giftie gie us
To see ourselves as others see us!

—*Robert Burns*

Many executives feel that personality assessment tools are a great waste of time and money. I disagree. From my extensive experience as a leader of both American and international organizations, I have learned that personality assessment tools, used in combination with good judgment and a bit of honest skepticism, can be helpful to the leader in a number of important ways.

First, personality assessment tools can help you to understand that other styles and other ways of dealing with situations are not wrong—they are just different from what you might have done. Too many leaders think that different perspectives are erroneous perspectives and, as a result, these executives fail to fully capitalize on the strengths of those who seem a little "different" or "strange." Second, these tools can help you realize the need for a diversity of personalities on the team. Diversity compensates for individual weaknesses and biases. It stretches the mind and reveals new possibilities and opportunities. Third, by better understanding people through personality assessment techniques, you often can assign associates to positions in which their personality traits will be most productive. The better personality assessment tools provide a framework to better serve the most important element of any organization—the people. Finally, these tools can be quite useful in the self-analysis and introspection process that every leader should undertake periodically. (For more information on personal introspection, see Chapter 16 and Appendix A, Checklist #12.)

An important part of many executive development courses is an assessment activity that administers a series of sophisticated tests. These tests are designed to evaluate the various skills, personality preferences, and leadership styles of the participants. The assessments offer the participants a unique set of insights into their various strengths and weaknesses. The courses then afford them the opportunity to learn new skills which help to promote their strengths and to correct their weaknesses. One of the most popular assessment instruments, and my personal favorite, is the Myers Briggs Type Indicator (MBTI).

The MBTI is based upon the typology of Carl Jung. The instrument measures personality styles and preferences along four continuums, which further separate into sixteen categories. The categories continue to differentiate according to the strengths of an individual's scores. The first continuum evaluates the individual in terms of extroversion or introversion. Jung, who coined these two terms, felt that this continuum represented the most powerful differences between people. The *extrovert* (E) thinks out loud in the world of people and things, while the *introvert* (I) processes information internally in the world of concepts and ideas.

The second division in the MBTI deals with the ways that individuals gather information for the decision-making process. There are two categories. One is called *sensing* (S), because people who fall into this type gather data with the five basic senses. The other category is referred to as *intuition* (N), as those who are "N" personalities prefer to leap over the tangibles and look for hidden meanings, relationships, and possibilities.

The third section of the MBTI test assesses ways of deciding. People who make decisions fairly impersonally, basing them upon an evaluation of cause and effect, are categorized as *thinking* (T). Others tend to make decisions based on personal values, and these individuals are labeled as *feeling* (F).

The fourth and final continuum of the MBTI is the only dimension that is not directly drawn from Jungian theory, although it certainly complements it. This continuum, developed by the two authors of the MBTI, addresses the differences between people in their use of perception and their use of judgment when dealing with the outer world. Individuals who follow the *judging* (J) preference rely on a judging process, and tend to live in a planned, decided, orderly manner. They constantly seek to regulate and control their lives. In contrast, *perceptive* (P) individuals rely mainly on a perceptive process, living in a flexible and spontaneous manner. Their quest is to understand the meaning of life and to adapt to it. The various combinations of these four continuums make up the sixteen MBTI types. The table on page 106, taken from *Please Understand Me: An Essay on Temperament Styles* by David Keirsey and Marilyn Bates, illustrates the differences that are measured by the MBTI.

I am an "ENTJ" and have learned, over the years, the strengths and weaknesses of someone like me. I am a strong extrovert (E) and also strongly intuitive (N), as well as a thinker (T) and a judger (J). My biggest weakness as a leader is my extroversion; I tend to be a poor listener, since I love to talk. My second biggest weakness relates to the fact that I am a *T* rather than an *F*. Some people find me cold and uncaring—poor qualities for a leader.

Another useful test is the *Strength Deployment Inventory* (SDI), created by Dr. Elias H. Porter. This assessment tool will provide additional insight into your individual behavior and the behavior of others. The test measures behavior first under normal, stress-free conditions, and then when the individual is criticized. What is fascinating to me is that approximately 80 percent of us change our personalities when we are told that we are wrong or have made a mistake. The SDI indicates interpersonal styles clustered around the following orientations: altruistic-nurturing; analytic; assertive-directing; and flexible.

MBTI: Personality Styles and Preferences

E (75% of the population)	*versus*	**I (25% of the population)**
Sociability		Territoriality
Interaction		Concentration
External		Internal
Breadth		Depth
Extensive		Intensive
Multiplicity of relationships		Limited relationships
Expenditure of energies		Conservation of energies
Interest in external events		Interest in internal reaction

S (75% of the population)	*versus*	**N (25% of the population)**
Experience		Hunches
Past		Future
Realistic		Speculative
Perspiration		Inspiration
Actual		Possible
Down-to-earth		Head-in-clouds
Utility		Fantasy
Fact		Fiction
Practicality		Ingenuity
Sensible		Imaginative

T (50% of the population)	*versus*	**F (50% of the population)**
Objective		Subjective
Principles		Values
Policy		Social values
Laws		Extenuating circumstances
Criterion		Intimacy
Firmness		Persuasion
Impersonal		Personal
Justice		Humane
Categories		Harmony
Standards		Good or bad
Critique		Appreciate
Analysis		Sympathy
Allocation		Devotion

J (50% of the population)	*versus*	**P (50% of the population)**
Settled		Pending
Decided		Gather more data
Fixed		Flexible
Plan ahead		Adapt as you go
Run one's life		Let life happen
Closure		Open options
Decision-making		Treasure-hunting
Planned		Open ended
Completed		Emergent
Decisive		Tentative
Wrap it up		Something will turn up
Urgency		There's plenty of time
Deadline!		What deadline?
Get show on the road		Let's wait and see

The basic value system of an *altruistic-nurturing* individual is a genuine concern for the protection, growth, and personal welfare of others. He or she strives to be open and responsive to the needs of others. This style is color coded blue. Nurses and elementary school teachers often score as blue. I have a friend in Augusta, Georgia, who seems to be the ideal as a blue leader. Martha Scroggs has held a number of leadership and teaching positions in a parochial school (preschool through the eighth grade). For many years she stood at the school's front door from 7:30 a.m. to 8:15 a.m., meeting and greeting 400 enthusiastic children by name as they piled out of their cars, vans, and buses. She is also the official tooth-puller, having pulled more than 1,000 baby teeth over the years. Children, with parents in hand, willingly come to see her at night and on weekends when the tooth or teeth are "ready for Mrs. Scroggs." She does all this for the sheer joy of being with small children, and her "blueness" helps make her a particularly effective leader. Because of the nurturing and giving tendencies of this type, some may feel that a "blue" cannot be a strong leader, but that is not the case at all. For instance, the United States Marine Corps, a service well-respected for its fine leadership, has a very large number of individuals who fall under the blue code.

An *analytic* person values the importance of a rational, analytical process and order. His or her style is to be objective, in control of emotions, cautious, thorough, fair, and principled—to think things through before acting. Green is the code color for this type. Systems analysts, auditors, and budget experts often score as green.

The primary value system of an *assertive-directing* individual is a concern for task accomplishment, including the organization of people and associated resources toward that end. This style is geared toward leadership and persuasion, awareness of opportunities, the right to claim earned rewards quickly, and an inclination to push for immediate action. An assertive-directing person will challenge others and will relish risk-taking. This SDI code color for this orientation is red. Army, Navy, and Air Force officers, as well as corporate executives, often score as red.

Finally, the *flexible* individual displays a blend of the other three styles. He or she is not identified by a color, but is referred to as a *hub* (or a *rainbow*), as elements of all three of the above styles can be found within this person. A hub focuses on the importance of membership in groups and effective group behavior. He or she is open-minded, curious about what others think and feel, and willing to adapt and change. Such an individual likes to experiment with how to act, enjoys being a member of groups, and is recognized for his or her flexibility.

The Strength Deployment Inventory is useful because it categorizes individual orientations into groupings that are easy to understand. In my judgment, the most interesting insight that comes out of the SDI is what happens to individuals when they are confronted or criticized. Behavior orientation often changes. For instance, I am basically red-blue. That means I am a hard-driving, ambitious, goal-setting person, but that I also have some caring, altruistic qualities. My goal-setting qualities are more prominent than the altruistic qualities. When confronted, however, I adopt the analytical orientation (green); instead of becoming angered by criticism, I get interested. As a result, I handle criticism less emotionally than people who "turn red" and become angry when they are confronted.

Individuals who work hard to accommodate criticism, to compromise, and to find ways to end the confrontation as soon as possible are "blue reactors." If they cannot find accommodation, they will try to withdraw. The best example of a blue reactor that I know is Bill Clinton. I had two private meetings with Clinton, one a few months before he assumed the Presidency, and another at the three year mark in his first administration. He was interested in gaining insights about his role as Commander in Chief. President Clinton was extremely charming, listened intently, and seemed genuinely taken by my criticisms and excited about my suggestions. I left each meeting convinced that he would implement some of my recommended initiatives. Nothing whatsoever happened. He nurtured my criticisms but misled me into believing that he would implement my suggestions.

Perhaps the best public example of Clinton as a blue reactor occurred two years into his first term. With much urging from Hillary Clinton and Vice President Al Gore, Clinton decided that he must fire his press aide, Dee Dee Myers. She simply was not up to the extraordinary demands of this position. When he called her into his office to tell her his decision, a long discussion took place in which she made the case that she was capable of doing great work. Instead of firing her, Clinton actually promoted her, even though he knew that she was failing in her job. This is a classic case of a blue reactor. In fairness to Clinton, he realized that he was changing his mind (depending on who was the last person to meet with him) too much. He understood that he needed a tough-minded Chief of Staff to help him maintain some consistency in his decision-making. Again, with some urging from Hillary Clinton and Al Gore, he removed his old school chum Mack McLarty, and brought in Leon Panetta. Panetta and others who served as Chiefs of Staff helped hold President Clinton's feet to the fire and the consistency of presidential decision-making improved.

A third test which I find fascinating is the *hot reactor test*, which measures the relationship between psychological and physiological anxiety. The procedure takes about forty-five minutes to administer and assesses the relationship between stress and blood pressure. The subject is connected to an automatic blood pressure machine, and is then asked to engage in a series of mental activities. During these psychological exercises, a significant number of individuals exhibit blood pressure levels that are substantially higher than their resting blood pressures; research shows that when placed under mild psychological stress, about 25 percent of American executives react with very high blood pressure. The hot reactor test gives the subject an indication of how his or her body responds to stressful daily activities. Leaders who know how to apply data from the hot reactor test can do a great service for those associates who suffer major physical repercussions as a result of their reactions to ringing telephones, angry bosses, short deadlines, etc. These individuals can be helped with medical interventions and with lifestyle and work pattern changes. As a leader who is committed to the wellness of your staff, you may wish to learn about the hot reactor test and, if possible, make it available to your associates.

For years, research has proven that physical and mental health are closely related. Health testing, like personality assessment tools, can provide leaders with valuable information. People who are in regular exercise programs and who maintain good control of their work habits and diet often make greater long-term contributions to the organization than those who do not pay proper attention to their health and work practices and, therefore, often don't reach potential performance levels. Treadmill stress tests, in coordination with a blood chemistry analysis, can determine quite precisely the "health age" of an individual. A fifty-year-old person who has a health age of sixty-five may not contribute to an organization for many more years unless corrective action with regard to diet, exercise, and excessive smoking and/or drinking is taken soon. You should take these tests as well, since the health of the leader has a great deal to do with the health of the organization. Furthermore, by taking the tests, you demonstrate that you are a leader who holds interest in and support for the wellness program.

Physical and mental vigor have everything to do with physical and mental health. This is evident by the fact that many people do their best thinking while walking or jogging. They return from their exercise with renewed energy and vibrant ideas, thus better able to tackle the issues and tasks of the day. A leader who makes a visible commitment to an exercise program is likely to encourage others to make greater efforts toward fitness and wellness.

Every couple of weeks, as I welcome each new group of people that comes to work for me, I say, "If I see you walking down the hall with an athletic bag in your hand, that is good, not bad; take a few hours off each week for some vigorous exercise. You will be more productive in the long run." Look carefully at the exercise facilities and opportunities available to the men and women who work for your organization: locker rooms; shower facilities; exercise rooms; and intramural sports programs. Attention to this area can reap great benefits in performance and morale.

While developing an organizational climate that emphasizes good mental and physical health, every leader should be mindful of the needs of the physically challenged. As you set up exercise rooms, sports programs, aerobics classes, treadmill testing, etc., also plan comparable programs for the blind, the deaf, those confined to wheelchairs, and others whose needs may not be served by the standard company wellness program.

16
LOOKING AT YOURSELF
the importance of introspection

I worry about the self-made man who worships his maker.
—*Bishop Albert Stewart*

Half the CEOs of the world are below average.
—*David Campbell*

Picture yourself surrounded by mirrors of many kinds. Some of the mirrors provide accurate reflections so that you can judge correctly your work as leader. But a good number of the mirrors distort your image. Even the most consistent of leaders is understood in many different ways by many different people. Try to correct the worst of these distortions, whenever possible. However, it is important to avoid becoming paranoid or defensive concerning misperceptions about you that cannot be corrected. Inevitably, you will be happy with the reflection in some mirrors, and unhappy with the images in others. Herein lies the need for self-confidence, combined with the willingness to listen, to accept criticism, and to learn from mistakes.

As briefly discussed in Chapter 1, you are really five people: you are who you are; who you think you are; who your subordinates think you are; who your peers think you are; and who your superiors think you are. In many cases, there is a close relationship between and among the five "yous." Yet in other cases, the relationship is not close at all. Just as your qualities will be over-estimated or exaggerated in certain situations—you are probably not as good-looking, sexy, brilliant, witty, or charismatic as you sometimes think you are—there are times when you will be perceived, by yourself or by others, in much less favorable light than deserved. If, on a rare occasion, you have one too many drinks, you might be seen as a chronic alcoholic. If, once in a while, you close your eyes or nod off during a long, boring meeting, you could be understood as suffering from incipient senility. If you fire an associate, you might be misinterpreted as a heavy-fisted leader who uses termination to express authority. Mature leaders are aware of these "perception gaps." They work hard to become introspective, to separate what's real from what's not, to get feedback, and to take corrective action when appropriate.

Perhaps the greatest benefit to be gained from objective introspection is the resulting enhancement of executive performance. A leader who knows who he or she is, who recognizes and maximizes strengths, and who understands and compensates for weaknesses performs much better than a leader who does not (or cannot) understand himself or herself. Through self-analysis, some mistakes can be avoided completely. Furthermore, an introspective leader builds an aura of self-confidence that gains the respect of associates. The introspection process should be accomplished systematically, regularly, and with the help of someone else. There are professionals who can be very helpful in making your introspection meaningful. For instance, the Center for Creative Leadership in Greensboro, North Carolina, specializes in helping leaders maximize the value of introspection.

Part of self-evaluation is listening to what you say and how you say it, as well as anticipating how your phrases and messages will be received throughout the warp and woof of your organization. Try to avoid using phrases that send misleading or erroneous messages or that diminish the dignity of your associates, your organization, or yourself. Commonly used phrases, like "my door is always open" and "I never want to be surprised" may be fine for leaders of smaller organizations, but are likely to be very counterproductive for leaders of large organizations. Checklist #13 in Appendix A lists a number of phrases that top executives should avoid using because they send out misleading signals, reduce the dignity of the organization, establish an atmosphere of intimidation, or demonstrate a propensity towards micromanagement.

Knowing yourself, your ideals, and your psychological, spiritual, and religious strengths and weaknesses can help improve your ability to provide enlightened leadership. It is healthy and useful periodically to ask yourself questions such as: "To what values do I *really* think are worth committing myself?"; "What are my most deeply held prejudices?"; "Do I 'walk my talk'?"; "Do I *really* practice what I preach?" An executive needs to be introspective in order to avoid eventually becoming out of touch, arrogantly overbearing, or somewhat irrelevant and, hence, less effective as a leader. Self-evaluation involves assessing your on-the-job effectiveness. To begin, consider the suggestions and questions discussed in the balance of this chapter.

Establish your schedule. How much time do you spend visiting on the shop floor, in the manufacturing or maintenance areas, or in the field? Does your secretary keep a close track of your schedule and provide feedback as to how many hours each month you are spending in such aspects of your job? How many hours are you spending visiting other units or parts of the organization? What kinds of meetings do you attend, and who else takes part in those meetings? In my view, the four-hour rule—leaders should spend no more than four hours a day in the office—has great merit. The rest of the time should be spent meeting with other people, visiting subsidiary organizations, conducting ceremonies, or giving short, substantive motivational speeches.

Establish your priorities. Are your priorities clearly understood? Have you written them down and discussed them with your associates? Do you follow your own priorities? There should be a close correlation between the priorities of the leader and those of the organization. After these priorities are articulated in both oral and written form, you should follow them faithfully. If you establish an agenda that you are unwilling to follow, your actions will become the source of cynical comment.

Examine your reliability. How often do you cancel out of a meeting, speech, ceremony, visit, sporting event, or social engagement at the last minute? Once you make a commitment to do something, you should do it. Only an emergency or ill health should cause you to cancel. Of course, an important part of being reliable is being careful not to over-schedule yourself, not to accept responsibilities that you cannot fulfill, and not to doublebook a specific period.

In recent years, I have been impressed by the reliability and character of Colin Powell. Whenever he agrees to do something, he does it. Whenever I write to him, I always get an answer, and usually within a few days. General Powell is part of my integrity brain trust; every year or so, I seek his input on an integrity issue with which I am struggling. I can always count on him to return the call and to be very candid in his advice. Many people have commented on Powell's charisma, self-confidence, and speaking style. His extraordinary negotiation skills, his ability to think and act strategically, his integrity, and his reliability put him at the top of my list of role models for leaders to emulate.

Who tells you all the news—good and bad? It is important to have close-by people who are honest and forthright, who give you the bad news as well as the good news, and who are not bootlickers or apple polishers. The best leaders foster, in their associates, a willingness to tell the boss what they think and not what the boss thinks. You need to sit down periodically and ask yourself: "Who around me is willing to tell the full story?" Is it your deputy, your executive assistant, your secretary, a trusted friend, your spouse, or your children? If there is no one, or if your truth-tellers' voices are very weak, you should hire someone to watch and report to you. Ultimately, you need to position him or her very close to you so that you have someone to tell you when the "emperor has no clothes."

How long are your meetings? If you love to hear your own voice, your meetings can go on for hours and can waste an enormous amount of time. Meetings should be short, brisk, and to the point, following a reasonable agenda set ahead of time. A good basic rule on routine meetings is that they should last no more than one hour. If there is to be a briefing, use no more than twenty slides. When there is more than an hour's worth of business to be done, the meeting should be broken into parts. Long meetings are wasteful, tying up people and straining many attendants' attention spans. You need to look at yourself and find out whether you have become, as many leaders do, enamored with your own words. Do you preach rather than listen?

How well do you listen? Listening is an acquired art. It requires self-discipline and well-developed skills. Leaders should listen and listen and listen; only through listening can they find out what's really going on. If an associate raises an issue and the leader does not allow the full case to be stated, the leader is likely to understand only a piece of the story and the problem probably will not be solved. In addition, the individual who brought the problem forward will be frustrated with the lack of opportunity to lay the whole issue on the table and to make sure the leader fully understood the problem.

Passive listening, where the leader listens quietly and does not interrupt with comments or questions, is appropriate in most cases. Active listening, in which the leader asks questions occasionally, also can be a useful way to keep track of what is being said. This ensures that there is a clear understanding of the case on both sides. It is a judgment call about whether the leader should be a passive listener or an active listener, but an effective leader is capable of doing both. When in doubt, err on the side of passive rather than active listening.

Do people fear you, distrust you, like you, respect you, love you? Are they comfortable with you or are they afraid of you? Do they withhold information for fear that you might explode, overreact, or make judgments about them that might be wrong? Do they feel free to tell it like it is? How people perceive you is important; if your coworkers feel good about you, respect and admire you, there will be better communication and, therefore, enhanced productivity. Do what you can to stay on comfortable and friendly terms, for it is difficult to break down boundaries once uneasy feelings have taken root. It is useful to remind yourself of the old adage: "Friends come and go, but enemies accumulate." Don't forget that good communication takes maintenance work. Your spouse, children, old friends, and trusted subordinates can help with this, being that they are very familiar with you and your communication skills. Like Ed Koch, the mayor of New York City for many years, you often should ask: "How am I doing?"

How is your body language? Do you exhibit a defensive nature? What is your office demeanor? Do you sit behind your desk and pontificate, or are you willing to step away from the seat of authority? Are you able, figuratively, to wrap your arms around people with warmth and concern? When discussing an issue with you, do associates feel that they can break through the interpersonal barriers that exist between subordinates and the boss? How approachable are you? Many leaders are visible, but not approachable. They don't realize how their demeanor makes people reluctant to approach them. A good leader commands a healthy respect without making others feel inferior or resentful. It is not necessary to build yourself up by tearing others down.

Are you considered to be a communicator? How well do you speak? Do you make brief speeches that are to the point, and do you include humor? How well and how often do you write? How well do you dictate and edit? If you do not master how to communicate with associates, you are more likely to be perceived as a figurehead, rather than as a true leader. A figurehead *maintains* a position; a true leader *guides and manages* from a position. Effective communication is a powerful means through which you can convince your coworkers that you are rightfully in a leadership role.

Are you considered to be a disciplinarian? If so, are you a benign or a harsh disciplinarian? Do you take time to counsel associates? Do you ever fire anyone? For what reasons and in what style? Do you warn and advise people before you relieve them of their responsibilities? Leaders who are tough but fair, who don't confuse leniency with leadership, normally serve their institutions well. Everyone respects a leader who is a fair disciplinarian, who does not fire without careful consideration, and who sets standards that he or she also is willing to maintain and uphold.

Do you enjoy your job? By letting people know that you are enjoying your job, you can help create a healthy atmosphere in your organization. Leaders who enjoy their jobs, and show everyone they do, often help their associates enjoy their jobs as well. Smiles and good words are usually contagious. Do you feel genuine joy in the successes of your subordinates? Let them know when you are pleased with their work and that you look forward to the workday because you're playing on a good team.

Are you an innovator? Are you someone who hangs on to the status quo? Are you dictated by policies that do not allow much flexibility? General Matthew Ridgway, the great combat leader of World War II and Korea, made a very telling point after he retired from the U.S. Army: "My greatest contribution as Chief of Staff was nourishing the mavericks." Are you someone who is open to suggestions, ideas, new thoughts, new directions, and new concepts? On the other hand, are you someone who innovates too much and creates turmoil within the organization because you are constantly changing your mind on policies, organizations, personnel, and other issues? Have you found the proper balance between continuity and creativity? In some situations, a great deal of innovation is needed and accepted. In other situations, innovation must be pushed slowly and incrementally to preserve the existing strength of the organization. To know the answer, you must know the organization.

Are you flexible? This question is related to the one above. Are you so rigid in your thinking and lifestyle that you are not open to new ideas? Conversely, are you flexible to a fault? Do you swing with the breeze? Where do you fit on the continuum between too much flexibility and not enough? You must use good judgment when it comes to being steadfast. Good leaders are not push-overs, nor are they tyrants. Through carefully observing and listening to the dynamics of the organization, you should be able to decipher how flexible you need to be. As is true with many issues, it is best to avoid extremes.

Do you maintain physical and intellectual fitness? Do you show some interest in maintaining physical fitness or are you too busy or too disinclined to get involved in sporting activities or an exercise program? It is in your interest, as a leader of an organization, to encourage people to take some time for physical fitness and recreation. If you are a nonathlete and you are not interested in fitness, you at least should understand that an athletic program may be very useful to the organization. Are you intellectually fit? Do you have a reading program? Do you bring in consultants and futurists to stretch your mind and the minds of your associates? Bodies and minds need frequent exercise to remain productive.

Are you a deflector of pressure from above or a magnifier of that pressure? One of your roles as a leader is to accept guidance and criticism in a mature way. If you are constantly magnifying the pressure that comes from your superiors, putting more and more pressure on your associates as a result, you may be doing a disservice to organizational morale and to your mission. At times, a leader should deflect these pressures; at other times, a leader should let some of these pressures flow through the organization. A good rule of thumb is to be a "heat shield" for any guidance and direction from above that will significantly damage your organization's ability to accomplish its goals or will cause serious and lasting morale problems. You may not be able to deflect all of the heat from the big boss, but you should deflect some of it.

Are you tuned in or are you out of touch? Leaders who isolate themselves in their offices or who don't have the ability to reach out and learn what's really happening soon get a reputation for being out of touch. What are the best means for staying tuned in? Are your antennae out all the time? Do you have good feedback mechanisms? A lot of problems develop when associates realize that the leaders are unfamiliar with or uninvolved in their work.

Some will be tempted to take advantage of the fact that they are not being observed carefully. Others will feel neglected and underappreciated because their leader does not seem concerned.

Are you a delegator? There are many bosses who run their entire organization from the front office. These tend to be individuals with enormous amounts of energy and intellect. Unfortunately, such individuals do not help associates develop into future leaders. Leaders who are willing to delegate authority are not only encouraging leadership at lower levels, but are also giving people a great deal of psychic reward. If you are willing to delegate rather liberally, you are probably doing a good job of creating a healthy organization that can carry on effectively if you should become disabled, incapacitated, or replaced by a less competent individual. A major aspect of delegation is empowerment. The top leader should empower associates so that they have full authority to make decisions without checking with the top leader. Many leaders delegate conditionally when they should empower unconditionally. However, caution should be taken. A leader should not be so aggressive in the desire to delegate that he or she loses touch and becomes nothing more than a traffic cop. Over-delegation can lead to the "Balkanization" of an organization, where no one is in charge.

Are you a nondrinker, a drinker, or an alcoholic? Occasionally, a leader who had a mild drinking problem prior to taking over leadership responsibilities drifts into a heavier drinking pattern that may lead to alcoholism. The pressures of leadership are sometimes quite severe, and individuals who have psychological or health problems relating to alcohol abuse often find their problems magnified. With regard to alcohol, you need to ask yourself some key questions: "Now that I'm a leader, what should be my approach to alcohol consumption?"; "How are my drinking habits viewed by others?" The perception of alcoholism in a leader is often as damaging as the reality of alcoholism.

Are you an optimist or a pessimist? If you are constantly optimistic, always wearing rose-colored glasses, you may lose the respect of associates because you are unable to acknowledge the weaker sides of your organization. Perhaps you refuse to see the tough problems. On the other hand, if you are constantly pessimistic and cynical, the organization's morale probably will suffer. A pragmatically optimistic individual who is not a starry-eyed dreamer, but who comes to work with a lot of enthusiasm and optimism, tends to be an effective and respected leader. Although a cynic might start out as a competent leader, cynicism and pessimism are soon likely to transfer negatively throughout the organization.

What are your ethics and values? Do you ever mention religious or moral values in your speeches or in your writings? When there is a funeral in your organization, are you ever asked to participate in the service? Have you ever been asked to stand up in front of a religious group and give a talk? Many associates will observe whether you are committed to a system of ethics and values. They will hope for a leader who shares their values. You should be wary, however, about the danger of seeming to impose your religious standards on others. Leaders who are, or appear to be, self-righteous often fail to gain or maintain good rapport with a large number of employees.

Are you a writer? Do you write a column in the weekly newspaper? How well do you write or endorse employee evaluations? Do you write letters and, if so, do you write them well and with style? If you are a poor writer, you may unintentionally harm your people in many ways. When it is time for you to write a letter of recommendation for someone who has done an excellent job for you and the letter lacks punch, you are failing that individual. If your evaluation reports are poorly written and do not highlight adequately the performance of your subordinate associates, you are doing a disservice to them. Find someone to help you with your writing—to edit it, "clean it up," make it more "punchy," make it clearer. If you learn to write well, you can better serve your organization and your efforts will be greatly appreciated. As John Kenneth Galbraith has written, "If you write well, you will automatically get attention."

Are you ambitious? Is your ambition geared toward yourself or your associates and organization? In what ways do your ambitions surface? In recent years, a number of people who have moved to top positions in our government have been so personally ambitious that they have forgotten that their first responsibilities are to the mission and goals of the organization and to the country. Ambitions must be focused on the organization, not just on the self. That way, everyone will benefit and rewards will be greater in the long run. Part of being a good leader is realizing that you are there to provide a service to the people, not vice versa. Therefore, your ambitions should be geared toward helping as much of the whole as possible, not just your own career.

Are you secure or are you insecure? If you are secure within yourself and are capable of accepting criticism well, you can serve as a mature leader in many different positions. If you are basically insecure and worry a great deal about your performance and abilities, you may have a more difficult task. In general, your sense of security should increase as your organization succeeds. Many initially insecure people can build their self-confidence over time and can become mature, successful leaders. The leader's spouse can be very helpful by praising the leader's strengths and accomplishments, particularly when praise and support are not coming from other sources. Conversely, a spouse can do much good by taking the leader down a peg or two if the leader's ego becomes overly inflated.

Are you a philanderer or a flirt? Some leaders pursue the thrills of conquest. Moral issues aside, you must recognize that you are being watched very carefully. If you are in business, you will be observed by your associates and, in many cases, by the media. If you are in government, the media often becomes an even larger factor. If you are in the military, you are being observed by your command post, security police, secretary, executive officer, and subordinates. The word quickly gets out that the boss is looking for the next liaison. Many leaders in government and politics, as well as a number in the business world and the nonprofit sectors, have seen their careers destroyed for the simple reason that they would not control their libido. A good example is when, in the late 1990s, a senior Air Force general lost his chance to become the Chairman of the Joint Chiefs of Staff because the Secretary of Defense and others learned the full story on the general's long-term sexual relationship with a married woman.

What is your integrity level? Leaders must realize that personal integrity and institutional integrity meet in the front office. If you have a commitment to integrity—if you talk about it, write about it, mean it, and live it—there is a good chance that institutional *and* personal integrity throughout the organization will remain high. If, however, you do not concern yourself with it and are willing to allow the rules to be bent, institutional integrity may degenerate rapidly. As a leader, your concern with integrity largely will determine the standards and pride of the entire organization.

Are you an intense individual or are you relaxed? What kind of demeanor do you project as you enter meetings, carry on conversations, and make speeches? Are you able to relax, or do the burdens and responsibilities of leadership cause you to have an intense air about you most of the time? Do you sit on the front edge of your chair? Do you interrupt people when they are trying to tell you something? These signals can help you determine your level of intensity and may help you evaluate whether your intensity adds to or detracts from your success as a leader.

Are you decisive or are you a "decision ducker"? A witty person once said that there are three types of people: those who make things happen, those who watch things happen, and those who wonder what happened. Heed the words of Johann Schiller: "He who considers too much will perform too little." Top leaders should follow the 60-percent rule—when you have about 60 percent of the information that you need to make a decision, you should make it, because if you wait much longer to get more information, your decision will come too late. Be a leader who makes things happen.

Leaders who constantly duck decisions create atmospheres of indecision. Such a climate tends to cause the organization to drift. Too often, decisions that should be made by the boss end up being made by lower-level associates without full coordination. If top-level decisions are always left to associates, consistency and coherency of policy will suffer, even though many of those decisions may be good. If you prefer to have subordinate associates make most of the decisions, at least ensure that there are general rules of policy and coordination that apply to all decision-making processes.

How "conceptual" are you? Are you able to put the mission, goals, requirements, and responsibilities of the organization into a conceptual framework? Are you able to explain that framework to other people? A leader who conceptualizes well is usually a good planner and an excellent teacher. It is important to provide a comprehensive "big picture" that explains the visions, goals, and priorities of the organization.

Avoid executive malaise. Most leaders do not reach positions of great responsibility until they reach their forties or early fifties. While climbing up the executive ladder, many of these leaders have worked very long hours, with little time for a systematic physical exercise program. They may have developed poor dietary habits; perhaps they have become heavy smokers or drinkers. Executive burnout is a rather common phenomenon for individuals of this type. This burnout can be avoided by careful time management, good control of diet and smoking, and a regular fitness program in which vigorous exercise, three or four times a week, becomes an integral part of the weekly schedule. Another aspect of executive malaise is the tendency of some leaders to be seduced by "perks." Company airplanes, board memberships, magnificent offices, superb outer-office support, and travel opportunities can subtly divert the leader's attention from the mission.

Although it is unpleasant to admit, a certain amount of executive malaise naturally comes with age. Let's consider military leadership. J.F.C. Fuller's classic book, *Generalship: Its*

Diseases and Their Cures, makes the point that, in war, the best generalship is performed by leaders between the ages of thirty-four and forty-five. This is due to the fact that combat leadership requires the physical strength, courage, stamina, flexibility, and risk-taking skills seldom found in men past the age of fifty. In gathering his information, Fuller examined 100 great military leaders of history and found that at the time of their greatest triumph, they tended to be quite young—74 percent were forty-five years old or younger. Although *Generalship: Its Diseases and Their Cures* was written before World War II, it supports the present personnel policy of the United States military, which has most senior officers retiring by their early fifties. However, leaders in their fifties and sixties can remain very effective if they maintain an intellectual, physical, and emotional fitness program.

Avoid both the Peter and the Paul Principles. The Peter Principle, whereby individuals tend to get promoted to their "level of incompetence" and then get stuck there, is easy to understand. Leaders must be careful to avoid the Peter Principle themselves, and to do their best to prevent it from becoming the norm in the organizations they lead. Promotion systems should concentrate heavily on *potential* and should be flexible enough so that when it is clear that people have reached their level of incompetence, steps can be taken to gently move them back to a position in which they can function effectively. Preparation for the increase in responsibilities that comes along with promotion is also important. If you are promoting an associate, make sure that he or she is fully aware of the extent of the new tasks.

The Paul Principle is a little more difficult to understand, but it can be almost as destructive to good leadership as the Peter Principle. The Paul Principle is the gradual obsolescence of leaders, as they lose touch with the organizations they lead, become too conservative, resist innovation and change, and fail to take advantage of technological breakthroughs. A systematic reading program, participation in management training symposia or workshops, regular interaction with long-range planners, and brainstorming activities with the staff can help to keep executives from falling into this insidious trap.

When I lecture on leadership and discuss the Paul Principle, I say, "Too many top leaders are brain dead." This comment almost always gets a laugh and some knowing nods. Why? Because it is fundamentally true; too many executives let their brains rest, when they should be using them actively and to their full potential. Leaders can overcome the Paul Principle if they maintain the kind of energetic commitment to creativity and innovation that they demonstrated on the way to the top. If, as a top executive, you are bored, tired, or looking forward to retirement, you should accelerate that decision; retire next month and let someone else take the reins! The fact that you worked long and hard to reach the top does not justify the attitude that the company owes you a number of years in semi-retirement as CEO. If you are burned-out, admit it and take early retirement. It is much better to leave a year too early, rather than a year or more too late.

A closely related problem is the "last-year syndrome." Unfortunately, some executives become bitter, cynical, and imperious during the last year at the top. This can be caused by a number of factors: the realization that all the goals that they had set for their organization will not be met; the understanding that they soon will give up all the trappings of power; the fear of the unknowns of retired life; the anticipation of withdrawal pains; the fact that age has crept up on them. As a leader approaches the final year, he or she should make a concerted effort to avoid this last-year syndrome. In some cases, the leader should decide to retire a year early and give the new team a chance to take charge. After all, no one will benefit if the leader is not functioning at his or her best.

Be aware of the red reactor problem. Those leaders who react emotionally or violently to criticism from below often fail as leaders because, over time, they lose touch with the most important and the most difficult issues. They also tend to lose some of their best people who, out of frustration, move on to other places where constructive criticism is part of the organizational climate. Leaders who take criticism poorly damage vital feedback mechanisms and may cause associates to jump ship. When such leaders face crises, they will look futilely for the creative associates who could have bailed them out. Over time, such leaders have difficulty recruiting talented individuals, for the word quickly spreads when a top leader is unreceptive to criticism. A particularly destructive quality in a leader is a tendency to hold grudges. Those individuals who know they are "red reactors" should strive to constrain this personality trait. At the same time, they should look for individuals with enough self-confidence not to be intimidated by an occasional outburst from the leader.

Know your people. How many people within a large organization should a leader know personally? A good general number is 500. Leaders should know well their immediate staff and their key associates throughout the organization. Added together, this number is likely to be between 50 and 100. Executives should also know a good number of people in the field offices, on the production line, in the legal office, in the financial office, in the marketing offices, etc. Furthermore, an effective leader is familiar with the important informal leaders, especially in the various minority groups. The top executive should acquaint himself or herself with the employees who are particularly outstanding, as well as those who are particularly troublesome. The executive should give each group some personal attention at various times. If the leader knows more than approximately 500 employees, he or she may be spending too much time learning (and retaining) names and too little time focusing on the important issues. On the other hand, if the leader knows fewer than 500 individuals, he or she may be losing touch with people who can provide valuable information, ideas, and insights.

"Do it all" leaders burn themselves out. "Delegate it all" leaders lose touch. "Sliders" postpone too many decisions. "Hyper ambitious" leaders spend too much time impressing the boss and depressing their followers. Wise leaders avoid these pitfalls through systematic introspection.

If, after going through the exercise of careful introspection, you decide that leadership is not your bag, it is best to begin to make preparation for other work. People who do not find leadership an uplifting and rewarding experience should not seek prominent leadership jobs, and should not stay in them if they are already at the top. Honest introspection can help you decide whether or not you can march enthusiastically to the beat of the leadership drum.

17

LEADING IN CRISES
coolness and flexibility

*The Chinese use two brush strokes to write the word "crisis."
One brush stroke stands for danger, the other for opportunity.
In a crisis, be aware of the danger—but recognize the opportunity.*

—Richard M. Nixon

The only way I know to handle failure is to gain historical perspective, to think about men who have successfully lived with failure in our religious and classical past.

—James Stockdale

All of us live in a high-pressure world; it is not just the mayors of major cities, police and fire department chiefs, hospital emergency room staff, and military leaders who have to deal with crisis situations. Business leaders must be prepared for such diverse and threatening emergencies as the poisoning of drugs, the leakage of nuclear radiation or toxic gases, airplane crashes, hostile corporate takeover attempts, stock market crashes, etc. Although my personal experiences with crises have dealt largely with international incidents and war, many of my principles and guidelines apply quite well to difficult situations across the spectrum of business, nonprofit, government, and military activities.

No matter how well a leader plans, anticipates problems, and reacts in normal day-to-day activity, crises will occur. The enormity of a crisis, the time constraints, the fact that people's lives may be in danger, or other unique factors will present challenges that will test you severely. A crisis situation calls upon skills and leadership techniques that normally are not exercised. When your organization faces such a time, be aware that you will often be short on facts, that emotions may be running high, and that the "fog of war" will lead to much confusion. Even though none of the options will be ideal, you must be decisive.

Five major aspects of crisis leadership are decisiveness; flexibility; innovation; simplicity; and empowerment. You must be open to suggestions on how to solve crises, and be willing to allow emergent leaders to assist. A hallmark of crisis leadership is keeping things simple—asking associates to do things that they are already trained to do, and not asking them to do new things with which they are unfamiliar.

Some executives deal with crises on almost a day-to-day basis. A principal of a very large, racially and ethnically diverse high school in a suburban area near a large city shared with me many of the difficulties he has faced in recent years: suicides, attempted suicides, gang fights, severe drug incidents, sexual behavior between teachers and students, attempted rapes, etc. Executives in these kinds of situations need to plan carefully in anticipation of upcoming problems. Crisis response teams should be formed and ready. Quick access to police and fire departments, as well as to nearby hospitals, needs to be organized in advance. Principals must reach out to these agencies so that the officials will be responsive to their needs. Furthermore, principals and vice principals should be very visible and very approachable, so that they can be alerted ahead of time to conditions that students and faculty members find potentially threatening. Through quick action, such leaders can head off many crises and competently handle the ones that do develop.

When he hears of upcoming trouble, one technique that the above-discussed principal uses can be labeled *preemptive warning*. He starts spreading the word with tuned-in students—those who are basically supportive of school policies, but who are also in close personal contact with other students who may be planning disruptive activities—that he is aware of what is about to happen and will pass out severe punishment if it is carried out. Moreover, he puts the word out on what the punishment will be. If the act takes place, this principal delivers the punishment as advertised. This gives him a lot of credibility at a time of great tension, and often stops the activity from ever taking place. He also uses the language of the corridor to get his message across; without using profanity, he uses such terms as "If you do this, you are history," or, "You do this and it's the highway." My friend is not afraid to demonstrate his strong emotional commitment to his school and to his standards. Since most of his students are committed to his school and his program, his tough words and strong sense of concern have real impact, especially at times of high tension. His presence in the halls and at all the major sporting events provides not only support for student activities, but also a deterrent to disruptive or violent behavior. As evidenced by this man, an effective leader is more than a good crisis manager; he or she anticipates and heads off crises.

In many acute crises, such as natural disasters, fires, and industrial explosions, as well as in crises normally associated with the military, such as terrorist acts, low-intensity conflict, and war, a leader may not have the communications on hand to be able to manage the situation. Additionally, he or she may be isolated from the crisis (for example, taken hostage), be injured, have had a heart attack, or be incapacitated for other reasons. In anticipation of crises, identify and train other leaders who can pick up the ball and handle the problems.

The crisis manager must be technically competent and must understand the people, the organization, the mission, the goals, and the priorities. You cannot operate with a superficial knowledge of what the organization is about and what its capabilities are. In a crisis situation, it is of utmost importance to remain calm and dispassionate. You must keep an eye on individual performances, while holding the mission as the first priority. Although emotionally involved in the issues, you must stand back from the situation and make the choices which ensure that the plan is carried out and the best possible solutions are achieved. In an extreme situation, that may mean sacrificing your or another's career, health, or life for the greater good of the largest number of people, or the greater good of the mission. Such situations often occur in combat.

The parallel between combat leadership and crisis leadership is close, although lives are not always endangered in the latter. There are the same tensions, the same need for flexibility and innovation, and the same demand to keep things basic and simple. The motivational leadership required in combat often is needed during non-combat crises as well, to ensure that individuals work in close harmony. In combat, soldiers believe that they have a real chance to succeed. They trust and respect their leaders, have feelings of individual invulnerability, and believe it will be the enemy who will die. During any type of crisis, those involved should have the same sense of confidence and security in the responses about to take place. This stems from the leader, who needs to operate in a well-trained, yet pragmatic way. You must not be tied inflexibly to the policies of the past, for they may not apply to the fast-moving conditions of the present.

A crisis often provides a very severe test of the horizontal and vertical cohesion of an organization. Organizations that are well-led, well-managed, in which the staff has worked hard to pull peer groups together (horizontal cohesion) and to ensure warm relationships between intermediate-level supervisors and their subordinates (vertical cohesion) often do well in a crisis. In fact, these organizations can be *strengthened* by a crisis, because many people learn from the experience and take pride that they have performed well during the stressful experience. For example, the Tylenol poisoning crisis actually made Johnson & Johnson stronger. The company performed quickly and maturely by pulling a huge amount of Tylenol off the shelves. The leaders remained calm and collected, refusing to overreact to criticism. Johnson & Johnson's public image was enhanced as it developed better anti-tampering devices for its drugs.

One of the most useful techniques for you to employ in a crisis is to develop an "opportunity team." This team should not be directly involved in the moment-by-moment management of the crisis, but should be close enough to the situation to be able to sit back, analyze opportunities, and suggest actions. Because leaders are so busy managing the crisis, they usually have no time to generate ideas concerning the accomplishment of things that could not be done under ordinary circumstances. A small, diverse group of innovators, perhaps the corporate long-range planning group, can provide the "Why don't we try this?" or "Have you thought of this option?" input. Thus, the organization can turn a crisis, which is both a challenge and a unique event, into an opportunity.

President John F. Kennedy's response to the Berlin Wall crisis of 1961 serves as an excellent example of a leader taking advantage of a crisis. Kennedy used that crisis as an opportunity to build up conventional military forces, to call reserves onto active duty, and to deploy units to Europe for training and deterrent value. He had an "opportunity plan" and he carried it out. Franklin Roosevelt also took advantage of various world crises in the late 1930s and early 1940s to help prepare the United States for war. His initiation of a peacetime draft, lend-lease, and the "destroyer deal" are three examples. The first initiative prepared the nation well for wartime needs, and the last two initiatives helped the British at a time when they were desperately in need of military equipment to deal with the German threat.

After a crisis is over, it is useful to conduct a "hot wash-up"—a wonderfully descriptive term used throughout the NATO Alliance—which brings together the key people involved in the crisis to analyze what lessons were learned. In addition, an after-action report, including an analysis of points or areas where future crises can be handled better, should be completed.

A caution is in order. Some leaders so thrive in a crisis environment that if one does not exist, they will often create one themselves! This can be a way of gaining the attention of lethargic employees and getting them to work at a high level of commitment and energy. But, on the other hand, creating crises can be quite disruptive and counterproductive. It can lead to cynicism and disgruntlement on the part of associates. Employees will roll their eyes up to the ceiling and say under their breaths, "Here we go again."

If you notice that, as a leader, you simply move from crisis to crisis, ask yourself how many of these crises are generated from within the organization itself. Who knows—it may be your associates creating crises just to keep you busy or happy, or you may be encouraging crises in order to spur on your own energy.

18

DEALING WITH THE MEDIA

the challenge and the opportunity

Just because you are paranoid doesn't mean that people aren't out to get you.

—Robert Pfaltzgraff

Truth is generally the best vindication against slander.

—Abraham Lincoln

Meeting the press fairly and squarely is a challenge of considerable proportions for leaders. Those who make it a policy to avoid contact with the media miss the chance to learn and grow from the crucible that an active free press provides. Even more importantly, the media offers an avenue through which leaders can compliment and thank others, and get proper recognition for their organizations and their people. Therefore, you should try to interest the media in writing stories and producing radio and television shows that support your organization's goals and highlight the accomplishments of the employees.

Refrain from the attitude that the media is the enemy or that the press cannot be trusted. In general, the media can be helpful. It is important, though, to maintain an attitude of skepticism because you occasionally may be burned by a member of the media. You cannot underestimate the importance of being accurate in what you say to journalists; avoid making statements that easily can be taken out of context or misquoted.

It is useful to establish ground rules with each media contact. Will the interview be on or off the record? Will you have the opportunity to see the manuscript or the videotape before it is released? If not, why not? It generally is useful to speak informally with the reporter before you get into the actual interview, in order to find out whether that reporter has any major preconceptions or misconceptions. If so, you can try to correct or rectify these before the interview begins. And if you cannot set things straight, be particularly wary of what you say. When media representatives have already made up their minds, it is often a question of trying to "limit damage" as much as possible. If a member of the media is clearly biased and is not likely to do a fair story, you have a responsibility to alert your bosses and the public affairs people at higher levels, to let them know that a critical article or program soon will appear, despite your best efforts.

If a reporter is willing to show the manuscript to you before it goes to press, you have a chance to clear up some misconceptions, to correct errors, or to expand some important points. Many responsible journalists will allow you to help them if you have established an atmosphere of mutual respect. Joking with the media, giving them the opportunity to observe firsthand what your organization does, and offering them the chance to see some things that they would not normally see and to talk to people with whom they would not normally have contact are some useful techniques to consider. These approaches can help to establish a positive rapport between you and influential news professionals, as well as to break down the natural barriers that often exist.

When a media visit is imminent, you can run stories in the company newspaper, telling the readers that CNN, *The New York Times*, or *The Economist* will be doing a story. Explain that the media's interest is a compliment. The presence of the media can be used as a motivating and uplifting experience for members of your organization. If you can get the word out ahead of time, you will communicate to the members of the press that you have alerted your associates that they are coming, that you are happy that they are there, and that you have encouraged candor in answering their questions. Consequently, this may spark a good long-term relationship with working members of the press.

Often, when media representatives interview a leader, they don't ask the best questions. If you feel comfortable with those who are asking the questions, you often can steer them in the right direction. For example, if the interviewer asks a question that is not particularly relevant, you can provide an answer and then say, "That was a good question, but I think there is a better question along the following lines." Then you ask the question and answer it yourself. This will educate the media representative, and he or she very well may pick up on your points. Thus, the interview will become more productive. Members of the media often spread themselves so thin across so many issues that they really don't know what questions to ask. You can help them ask the best questions. This technique puts you in charge of the interview and helps to tell the story you want to tell.

You should have an agenda and a theme or point of view that you want to get across during the interview. Your answers to the interviewer's questions should announce that agenda loud and clear. During a press interview with Donald Rumsfeld when he was Secretary of Defense, Rumsfeld was asked how his elderly mother was. Rumsfeld's reply was that she was fine, but that she was worried about the Russian threat! His witty answer took the direction of the interview right back to the type of discussion that Rumsfeld desired.

Leaders should consider the audience and empathize with their concerns about the issues at hand. Be straightforward in your answers to questions, and avoid jargon and technical language that may not be understood. If you don't know an answer to a question, the very best reply is "I don't know." I learned from my experience on CNN during the 1991 Gulf War that this answer is a good one for many reasons. First, it is an honest answer. Second, it allows you to get to the next question quickly. Third, if you "wing it" and guess, the follow-up questions on the same subject will often destroy your credibility. Very soon, it will be clear to the viewing audience that you don't know what you are talking about. In the winter and spring of 1991, I received hundreds of letters about my commentary on CNN. Many praised me for my honesty and for my willingness to say, rather often, that I did not know the answer to a specific question.

Members of the media are always looking for a news hook: something interesting on which to hang the story. A leader can help provide such hooks if he or she is sensitive to the needs of the press and, therefore, reaches out to their associates to get ideas on how to bring newsworthy issues to the attention of reporters. The flip side of this point is also true. A leader can use upcoming news conferences as a means to encourage associates to come up with courses of action that will benefit the organization. For instance, President Kennedy used his biweekly press conference to accelerate the decision-making process, to keep informed on current issues, and to make policy decisions.

Media speeches are significant events that afford much exposure. In fact, official speeches often are the most important means by which decisions are announced. Use these opportunities to their fullest advantages. Speechwriters can be useful instruments in the decision-making process. Therefore, it is important to foster a close relationship between your speechwriters and your public affairs specialists, so that interactions with the media and the general public can be as coherent as possible.

Some large organizations have a media-training program for senior executives that gives them a chance to face various media challenges in a well-simulated environment. During this training, the following practice sessions are videotaped: a one-on-one interview; a general news conference; a confrontational news conference; a remote interview; and a speech followed by a question-and-answer format. The executive is then critiqued on style, body language, sense of humor, speaking voice, etc. Individuals who expect to move into top executive positions should take this training.

Although some have argued that America has developed into a massive adversary culture in which the media's disparagement of all our institutions has become the norm, mature leaders can find ways to work positively with representatives of the news profession. Leaders of large organizations cannot hide from media representatives. These executives should meet often with their public affairs officers and seek their guidance, criticism, and support.

Finally and perhaps most importantly, leaders must ask

themselves honestly how firmly committed they are to freedom of the press and a robust first amendment. The leader who loves to be secretive, who feels the media is not a responsible element in society, or who is uncomfortable when in contact with members of the press is likely to be treated unfairly by the media. This treatment is often a result of a press representative's frustrated desire to have a full dialogue with the executive. On being thwarted by the leader's reluctance to be open, candid, and helpful, the reporter sometimes responds by writing a critical and biased article. Leaders of large organizations in all areas of society must understand that they will have some media attention and must conduct their personal and professional lives with that fact in mind.

19
SPOUSES OF THE LEADERSHIP TEAM
the delicate balance

One of the best hearing aids a man can have is an attentive wife.
—Groucho Marx

One of the more sensitive issues that leaders face in the current cultural environment is the extent of the spouse's supporting role. In some leadership situations, the spouse of the leader has a very small role to play, but in many others, the role can be and is quite important. Many spouses of leaders are of invaluable help as quiet supporters, critics, conduits for information, and sounding boards. Prince Philip responsibly supports Queen Elizabeth of England in her many administrative and ceremonial roles. Eleanor Roosevelt took an active part in President Franklin Delano Roosevelt's career, while making a striking impact in areas of her own interest. Spouses of leaders in many organizational settings would do well to emulate these two examples.

On the other hand, when a spouse is perceived as being involved in policy issues, the hiring and firing of key associates, etc., the effectiveness and morale of the organization often suffer. A leader should be sensitive to these concerns and should not allow the spouse, no matter how strong the personality, to influence policy. There have been many interesting case studies in the American political and economic system that seem to indicate the dangers of a spouse exercising an inordinate amount of power and influence. The situation involving Phillip Agee and Mary Cunningham at Bendix in the early 1980s, and the role of the President's wife in the Wilson, Harding, Carter, and Clinton Presidencies bring to mind the inherent dangers to the credibility of the leader when a spouse's influence extends far beyond the family circle.

Another sensitive issue, for many, is the role that spouses of the top leadership team play in supporting the activities of the organization. This subject can be fraught with so much emotion and residual hard feelings that some leaders prefer neither to discuss it nor to outline a policy position, either formal or informal, on the subject. From my experience in leading both line and staff organizations, and as a head of an academic institution, I have come to the conclusion that spouses of subordinate leaders should never be pressured to participate in activities that support the organization. However, those who choose to participate should be given full latitude to do so and should be thanked often for their willingness to be helpful. Perhaps a few examples will help illustrate my point.

A research company that has grown at a rate of 60 percent per year since it was started eight years ago has five major groups, each under a vice president. The Chairman of the Board has noticed that one of the groups has a very active social program led by the spouse of the vice president. Another group has no social program at all. The remaining groups are somewhere in between. The group with the active social program has the lowest turnover rate and the highest productivity rate. Recently, the employees and the spouses of this group pulled together, on a volunteer basis, to help one of their members with a severe health problem. They not only directly aided the ill person, but also helped draw attention to a little-known health problem that needed national attention. The entire organization took pride in the fact that the company was willing to be so helpful to someone in need. The Chairman of the Board has a definite philosophy regarding the social and supportive activities of the spouses in the various departments of his company. He never puts pressure on the subordinate leader or the spouse who does not participate, but he *privately* thanks the subordinate leader and the spouse who take part in an active program. He has noticed that the other groups are becoming more involved because of the "emulation effect." Rather than encouraging other vice presidents to do more, he is quite satisfied to watch informal emulation take place.

At overseas military bases, numerous young wives need support and assistance. Some of these women, many still in their teens, are homesick, unable to find work because of restrictive laws in the host country, living far away from the post without transportation, or living in very substandard housing because of the low pay that junior enlisted members of the armed services receive. The military can and does offer some official support, but it is often inadequate. Spouses of the leadership team can provide much help if they are willing to volunteer their time, energy, and creativity to build and sustain assistance programs.

The natural tendency to reach out and help people in need is often sufficient. In fact, in many cases, the only real requirement for the spouses of the key leaders is to show interest in and support for the activities that are already underway. However, in certain cases, this informal volunteer support structure does not exist or is so inadequate that the real needs are not being met. Under such circumstances, the leader is faced with a difficult dilemma. Employees are making strong, legitimate complaints that something must be done to support families in need. If the leader's spouse is able and willing, he or she can provide the leadership in forming groups and recruiting volunteers to assist. If the leader has no spouse, or if the spouse is unable or unwilling to take those reins, the issue becomes even more delicate. The leader must reach out and find someone else's spouse who is willing to lead the effort in building a voluntary support structure. The leader can do this in a number of ways. He or she can raise the issue during a staff meeting, write an editorial in the weekly newspaper, or talk about the problem at various social gatherings. The art of gentle persuasion, rather than the use of influence or pressure, is the best avenue. Once the willing spouse or spouses come forward, the top leader must donate time on the calendar to interact actively with these volunteers, to listen to ideas and feedback, and to give them guidance and support.

One of the big mistakes a leader can make is to put heavy pressure on the spouses of key associates to participate in these programs. Many spouses will resent this pushiness, while some will feel guilty about not properly supporting their spouses' careers. Very poor morale among the top leadership group can result. The leader should avoid the word "expect" when asking for the support of spouses. For instance, the seemingly benign appeal, "I realize that many of your spouses are busy working, raising families, and participating in volunteer activities outside the organizational environment, but I expect them to assist as much as they can," can be devastating or insulting to some husbands and wives. The word "expect" can be a very heavy term in this context. Many spouses will interpret this to mean that if they can't give a certain number of hours each week to these activities, their marriage partners' careers will be damaged. Some leaders make the mistake of establishing a policy that every spouse of every subordinate leader must get involved in activities that support the organization. The rationale is, "If everyone doesn't contribute, those that do will have to do more." Often, this rationale fails to take into account the voluntary nature of spouse involvement. It also is hopelessly out of date.

Heaps of private and public praise for those who help, a willingness to accept an informal support structure that may not be as strong as it might have been twenty or thirty years ago, and a resistance to the temptation to pressure spouses should be the ground rules for managing spouse participation. I have seen leaders fail badly when they or their spouses (or both) violated these ground rules, even though they had the best of intentions. Through heavy pressure, they built up impressive spouse support structures and, in so doing, they destroyed the morale of the top leadership group and did damage to the institution itself.

Try to put yourself in the position of the spouses of the subordinate leaders. You desperately want your husband or wife to be happy and successful, but you also have a very rewarding career that prevents heavy involvement in activities outside your own job environment. Or perhaps you are committed deeply to family, church, or charity efforts that lie outside the context of your spouse's organization. Imagining yourself in this position should make it evident that pressure from the big boss might very well impose a heavy emotional penalty on the entire family and, over time, may damage the performance of the subordinate leader.

Top leaders should be sensitive to the dangers of their spouses going on a "power trip" and turning active involvement of associates' spouses into a "loyalty check." I witnessed an extreme situation of this kind; in Europe, a specific colonel's wife occasionally would tell the wife of a junior officer, "I'll have your husband's job," if she didn't participate in some activity.

One technique that the World Bank uses to reward spouses for their patience and support is a point system. For every night that an official of the bank spends away from home, a point is awarded. After a certain number of points are earned, the spouse can travel with the employee at the expense of the World Bank. Hence, when the employee does travel, the spouse knows that points are being earned and particularly attractive trips together can be anticipated.

Everyone should realize that the supportive spouse is not always a wife. By serving as a sounding board, a source of quiet advice, a caring critic, and an instrument of direct feedback, the husband of a female leader can be an equally effective supporter. Fine models of recent times would be the husbands of the following prominent women: British Prime Minister Margaret Thatcher; Jeane Kirkpatrick, the former U.S. Representative to the United Nations; and, since 1996, Elizabeth Dole, the president of the American Red Cross.

It is essential that leaders continue to remind themselves that spouses seek fulfillment in their lives and have a perfect right to pursue their goals and dreams. If leaders are very supportive of their spouses, it is very likely that their spouses will, in turn, be supportive of the aspirations of the leaders.

20

LEADING INTERNATIONAL ORGANIZATIONS

dealing with cultural complexities and national antagonisms

Sometimes a man's fitness for a post of trust is determined by his associations.

—*Sidney Hook*

Leadership of international corporations or multinational government organizations is a particularly demanding responsibility. The leader should understand and be sensitive to cultural differences, national biases, antagonisms between and among national groups, and unusual administrative or bureaucratic processes. When an individual is going to move into a new situation involving the supervision of people from a number of nations, it is useful to do some background reading on each of those countries. Books on the history of specific nations offer many wonderful insights. I recommend Anthony Samson's work on England; Luigi Barzini's analysis of Italy; Gordon Craig's research on Germany; and Edwin Reischauer's study of Japan. Individuals from various nations are enormously complimented when their boss is able to speak knowledgeably about their history and their traditions. And the earlier the reading is done, the better.

Many large corporations have become extensively international, to the point at which employees, particularly the younger ones, think of themselves as international people with no strong ties to an individual nation. They become very mobile, are often proficient in two or more languages, and sometimes marry individuals from nations other than their own. Such trends are generally beneficial to the top leadership of these companies, for it is easier to move these associates around than to uproot those with strong emotional ties to one country. In addition, it is helpful because sometimes decisions must be made that are not in the national interest of particular countries. If the top corporate officers are associated too closely with an individual nation, they may not be able to make decisions as objectively as they should in serving their stockholders.

The international aspects of business, government, and the military are not without their problems. The host nation of the corporate headquarters may take a strong position on an issue that makes the corporate officers quite uncomfortable. Whether it be trade with Cuba, Iran, or Iraq, war with one or more countries, national conscription, or reserve military duty, leaders sometimes are faced with a set of bad choices. Government leaders must take into account the delicate position that multinational corporations face as they try to carry out their corporate decisions.

In every international organization, there will always be tensions with which the leader must deal. In my two years' experience in leading individuals from five nations (Great Britain, Germany, Belgium, the Netherlands, and the United States), I found that severe cross-national antagonisms existed. For instance, a few weeks after I moved into the organization, I asked a Dutch officer if he spelled his first name—Frans—with an "s" or a "z." With considerable anger, he replied that the *Germans* spelled it with a "z." If I had done my research, I would not have asked the question, for I would have known not only the answer, but also the Dutch-German sensitivities. Another example of the manifestation of this antagonism is illustrated by the fact that my German boss asked me to act as the disciplinarian for any Dutch or Belgian subordinate who needed counseling. My boss pointed out to me, "Everyone likes Americans, but some people don't like Germans."

In many cases, there are work-ethic differences between and among the nations in international organizations. For example, Americans tend to work long hours and to be quite concerned about deadlines. Europeans, on the other hand, are more likely to work less frenetically; they spend more time on the bigger issues and less time on the details. These differences cause morale problems on both sides. Individuals from nations that are accustomed to working short hours and to taking long lunch breaks tend to be critical of those who work longer and harder, and vice versa. It is important for the leader to establish a standard for work hours and to ensure that it is followed. Generally, the standard should be a compromise between the various extremes.

Language difficulties are very common in international organizations. As a result, the individuals who speak and write the language of the central headquarters have both a great advantage and a great burden. If English is the language of the organization, as is commonly the case, then the British, the Americans, the Canadians, and other English speakers will be expected to do most of the work—the writing, the speaking, and the briefing. The organization should not take advantage of or overwork these associates. Dealing with the other end of the problem, the leader must ensure that individuals who are not proficient at speaking and writing English are not removed from the decision-making process and are not neglected in staff activities. This is a very delicate issue. If they are assigned only the easy or noncontroversial tasks and problems, the leader will soon face a morale problem because those individuals will feel they are being pushed to the sidelines.

Although not normally a problem in business, in a governmental setting there may be large differences in the pay and allowances of employees with which the leader will have to deal. There may be civil servants and military officers working side by side with the same ranks or grade levels, but with major pay differences (as much as 100 percent). There is very little that the leader can do about this, but as activities (parties, receptions, and picnics) that require individuals to commit their personal funds are planned, it is important for the leader to be very sensitive to the fact that some people in the same job receive much less compensation.

Within every multinational governmental organization, there will be people from nations that are large, rich, and powerful, and others from nations that are smaller, poorer, and less powerful. The leader must understand the "small nation syndrome" and treat representatives of the latter with care. Substantive meetings should involve associates from all participating nations, even though the issue may have very little to do with one or two of the smaller countries. These nations deserve "a seat at the table." The leader must ensure that they always have a chair, for each individual represents a sovereign state despite differences in size or power.

Americans often become "bulls in china shops" when they join international organizations. The American way of attacking problems directly sometimes fails in an international setting. It is particularly important for American leaders of international organizations to be sensitive to various national concerns and to listen carefully to their advisers from various nations.

When you are about to take over an international organization, realize the importance of the transition process. You should ensure that the initial briefings are given, to a large extent, by individuals from nations other than your own. From the very beginning, your outer office should include secretaries, executive assistants, protocol officials, and public affairs and community relations specialists from various nations. In the course of day-to-day business, leaders of large international organizations should spend the great majority of their time with colleagues from other nations rather than with their national compatriots. This approach is important from the view of both substance and perception.

Would-be leaders of international corporations should try, as they move up in the company, to obtain positions that will enhance their understanding of other cultures. Overseas experience, language competence, and cultural sophistication can be very helpful when you become a leader of a large international organization. With these assets, you can reach out productively to people of many nations.

21
FIRING
the role of the leader

My wire was sent to get you to toughen up—to can these fellows who cannot produce. I want you to come out of this a real commander.

*—Letter from General Hap Arnold to
Lieutenant General Ira Eaker, Commander
Eighth Air Force in England
June 1943*

A leader must be able to look a man in the eye when he fires him and weep for him at the same time.

—James Stockdale

Leaders occasionally need to fire people. This occurs for a variety of reasons: to remove incompetents; to reinforce standards; to punish violations of integrity; etc. Generally, the leader should fire individuals himself or herself, and not delegate that task. If, however, a leader has a very large organization, some delegation may be necessary. In any case, people who work directly for the leader should be fired by the boss.

Before an individual is fired, it is your responsibility, as leader, to counsel the individual, in order to explain clearly where his or her job performance has been substandard. If, after a period of a few months, the performance standards still do not reach an acceptable level, seriously consider removing the individual from the position he or she holds. If you choose this course of action, meet personally with the associate. One approach is to tell the individual that you have lost confidence in his or her ability to do that job. During this session, it is important for you to give the associate who is being removed the opportunity to explain what problems exist and how he or she feels about this action. Be patient and be a passive listener. It is a very traumatic experience for an individual to be fired, for, in most cases, it will be the first time. You have a responsibility to help the employee work through this difficult experience. Let the employee know specifically that you are asking her or him to leave because you feel that it is your duty as a leader. It is also useful to point out that you understand that the employee will go through a difficult period in life (both personally, and with the family). You should talk at length to the individual about future prospects. If appropriate, offer to help in finding him or her a new position. You should explain that you will write a final effectiveness report or evaluation with care, to ensure that the individual's strengths are outlined just as fairly as his or her weaknesses.

I use a technique that has been of some help in easing the pain of the subordinate—I explain that I once was fired from a key job. I describe how this experience affected my family and me; I discuss the thoughts that went through my mind at the time it occurred and in the months that followed. Also, I point out that my next job turned out fine even though it was considered a poor one by my contemporaries. Most importantly, I emphasize that I learned a great deal from the experience and, in the long term, benefited from having experienced a major setback in my life. After all, I was able to move away from an impossible interpersonal situation with my boss and go to a place where I was welcome and where my talents were appreciated. I also relate how I was not told by my boss that I was being fired, nor had I been counselled by him ahead of time.

In some cases, the individual has failed so badly in performance, integrity, or some other area, that you must be quite tough on the final performance appraisal report. If the employee is being fired for cause (not just for substandard performance, but for a gross violation of integrity or extremely poor performance), there should be no question remaining in that employee's mind—or in the final report—about why he or she is being fired.

People often get fired because they are not doing a particular job well, but they still have talents and abilities that can be applied elsewhere. It is your responsibility, as a leader, to ensure that such individuals are moved into positions where they will have the opportunity to use and exploit their talents. You can help the transition into the new job by contacting the new boss, pointing out the strengths of the individual, and asking that the person be given a fresh start.

It is sometimes appropriate to suggest early retirement or a very significant job change. If the individual has demonstrated a real weakness in personal ability to do very basic things within the organization, it is best to be candid and suggest that retirement might be in order.

I have faced several different situations in my experience with firing individuals for specific reasons. When I was in charge of the National War College, there were thirty-five professors from various professional and academic backgrounds; some had tenure and others were there for three or four years. I had to remove a professor before the end of the academic year because I was getting bad feedback on his attitude, his teaching ability, and his failure to organize his courses properly. He had been counselled on a number of occasions by the Dean of Faculty, but there had been no improvement. In fact, his performance got worse. I met with him and explained the reasons why it was time for him to move on. We were able to find him a job where he was clearly competent. Although he was bitter about his experiences at the College and was not pleased with me, I think the move was best for him and certainly best for the College. If he had stayed at the College, there probably would have been further damage to his career due to his continuing failure to meet our expectations.

When I was running a large staff organization, I had to fire a man who was in charge of a planning division that consisted of ten professionals and two secretaries. He treated a group of talented and hardworking young people as if they were unreliable, immature, or both. He required them to check with him every time they left the office, even to grab a quick lunch or go to the restroom. He moved on to another job which took advantage of his creativity and energy, but where he had no one to supervise directly. He performed well.

On another occasion, I removed an Air Force colonel who was a base commander. He was in charge of about 800 individuals, including civil engineers, security police, and many other people responsible for the combat support of a tactical fighter wing in Europe. This man was married and lived with his wife on base; he had a girlfriend downtown. The colonel was using the military staff car to drive his girlfriend around Western Europe on weekends. He was embarrassing himself, his family, and the wing, since it was widely known that his girlfriend had moved to a nearby apartment. I told him that I could not tolerate that kind of activity, especially in light of strictly established policies that he, himself, was responsible for enforcing.

Another example of note would be the alcoholic who worked for me when I was at an international military headquarters in Northern Germany. He was from a small European nation. After some counselling by me and the senior officer from his country, I asked him to leave short of his normal tour of duty. It took a number of months before we could move him out because of the personnel system in his country. He was removed for chronic absenteeism and his unwillingness to face up to his problem and to seek or accept professional help.

A chief executive officer of a large research firm provided me with an interesting insight about employees who possess splendid educational credentials and highly developed technical skills. He has found that most employees who fit this description but are not performing up to standards are the first to realize it. It normally takes this CEO about three months to learn of the poor performance. By that time, the employees usually know that they are in trouble. The top executive then counsels them and gives them about six months to raise the performance level appreciably. If the employee realizes, in the next few months, that he or she will not be able to reach levels of expected performance, that individual often has already worked out some plans for the next job. Hence the departure interview usually can be accomplished without hard feelings and loss of friendship.

There are a number of subtleties to be considered when you make the decision to remove someone from a position.

A range of choices exists between a "hard" firing and a "soft" firing, and you should think through the various options quite carefully. Seek advice from your deputies, lawyers, and personnel directors (and from your expert on public relations, your psychiatrist, or your chaplain, where applicable). Before the individual who is to be removed from office is alerted of the termination, you must fully understand what authority is available, what the legal implications may be, how easy it will be to find a suitable replacement, etc. It also is wise to consider the impact on the performance and morale of the organization that may result from this action. See Checklist #5 in Appendix A for further guidelines on how to go about firing an employee.

Through a situation that I will regret for the rest of my life, let me explain the dangers of *not* firing someone when it is necessary. Many years ago, when I was a squadron fighter pilot and flight leader, there was a young pilot in my flight who was having considerable difficulties mastering the skills of air-to-ground combat. Since his progress was very slow, I considered recommending to my boss that he be grounded. However, the young man was so eager to be a successful fighter pilot—it had been a lifelong dream—that I chose to remain silent. A few months later, when I was leading a flight on the bombing range, he was flying in the number two position on my wing. As I pulled off the target on my first pass, I looked over my shoulder and watched as he rolled in to drop a small practice bomb on the target. He dived in at the normal 45° angle, but released his bomb late. During his pullout, which was also late, he hit the ground. He was flying at approximately 500 miles per hour when he crashed. The young pilot was killed instantly and the aircraft was completely destroyed. His death left a wife and two small children in grief. If I had done the right thing and grounded him, I would have saved his life.

Leaders who never fire anyone may be doing a disservice to their institution. Many people take advantage when they know that they are safe from the real discipline of being removed from their positions. Therefore, a deserved firing is not only the right thing to do, but it also sets the tone that there are certain standards of performance and ethics to be met. It is an important part of any leader's responsibility to fire the individuals who, *after proper counselling,* fail to live up to the organization's standards. Remember, a good leader always conducts those unpleasant sessions with compassion and dignity.

22

DEALING WITH THE DOWNSIDE

failures, rumors, criticism, and stepping down

Don't be discouraged by a failure. It can be a positive experience. Failure is, in a sense, the highway to success, inasmuch as every discovery of what is false leads us to seek earnestly after what is true, and every fresh experience points out some form of error which we shall afterwards carefully avoid.

> *—John Keats*

A thick skin is a gift of God.
> *—Conrad Adenauer*

When I was asked to speak to the Class of 2001 at one of the service academies, I assumed I would be asked to speak on leadership, or perhaps about my role as CNN's military analyst. To my surprise, the topic selected was "Dealing with Failure." I think I was chosen to address this subject because I had four major setbacks in the first twenty-two years of my military career. One of the most important qualities of a good leader is the capacity to deal constructively with setbacks and failure. Having failed many times as a leader, I have learned that failure is a marvelous learning and growing experience. I also have learned to tolerate the failures of my associates, since I can empathize with their experiences.

One of my failures occurred when I was fired from a key position in the Pentagon. As an Air Force colonel, I was serving as a military assistant to the Deputy Secretary of Defense. Since the Secretary of Defense is so busy dealing with Congress, the White House, the State Department, and the media, it is the Deputy Secretary of Defense who runs the Pentagon day by day. My job was to attend meetings with the Deputy Secretary and to travel with him. I was supposed to take notes and to ensure that his decisions were carried out faithfully and promptly. I also had the responsibility to tell him privately when I thought he was getting bad advice and when he was about to make a decision that might backfire on him.

One day, I got a call from a friend who was responsible for all assignments for Air Force colonels. He told me that I had just received a new assignment and was being sent to Europe to be the Chief of Maintenance for a fighter wing in Germany. This was quite curious news since I had been working for the Deputy Secretary for only eleven months. (The normal assignment was two years.) When I asked this personnel officer what the surprise assignment meant, he said, "Perry, you are history, you're toast. It's the highway for you, my friend." The next morning, I asked the Deputy Secretary to explain what was happening to me. He lied, saying that the Air Force wanted to get me back to airplanes and that, reluctantly, he was willing to let me go.

Most of my friends were convinced the my career was finished. They believed that I would never get another good assignment. Also, they hinted to me that there was no chance I would be considered for future promotion. It was the first major setback in my life, not to mention a wonderful lesson in humility. My family was very supportive. Fortunately, my wife was happy to get me away from a frustrating job, and my two teenage children were anxious to live in Europe. Soon, I was focusing my full attention on preparing for my next job and getting the family packed up for the flight across the Atlantic.

Within a few weeks, something curious began to happen. Some people were suggesting that my being fired was a blessing. The senior leadership in the Air Force did not respect the Deputy Secretary of Defense, and some of these top leaders felt that my being fired was a plus and not a minus—almost a badge of honor. Within two years of the date I was fired, I was given the best job in the Air Force, the command of the only F-15 wing in Europe. But, alas, that assignment also would lead to massive failure.

I had 4,000 people working for me at the time, and our job was to defend Western Europe from air attack. The military threat was from the Warsaw Pact countries to the east. These countries had a much larger number of combat aircraft than did NATO, so our job was especially challenging. As commander of the wing of eighty F-15s, I was responsible for conducting realistic training, for developing tactics for this wonderful new airplane, and for insuring that the flying operation was conducted professionally and safely.

During a period of nine months, five of our brand-new F-15s crashed. At that time, these airplanes cost about $20 million each. The problems were myriad, but they centered around two issues: the F-100 engine kept flaming out in flight, and the fuel system was faulty. Two weeks after the fifth airplane crashed, I learned, to my utter amazement, that the Air Force had promoted me from Colonel to Brigadier General. Normally, a wing commander is fired if he loses more than two airplanes; I had lost five.

About a month after my promotion was announced, I asked the commander of all U.S. Air Forces in Europe how I could possibly have been selected for promotion. The answer I got was fascinating; he replied, "Because you handled failure well." When I told him that I didn't understand what he meant, he told me that each wing commander was failing in one way or another. One had a major drug problem on his base, another had flunked a major NATO inspection, a third commander had a significant racial problem on his base, and yet another had a terrible ground-safety record. He then explained that he learns more of the character of leaders while they are dealing with failure than when they are succeeding. History supports this viewpoint that good leaders turn failures into constructive experiences. As I survey the great leaders of the past, many of them suffered setback after setback before they emerged as extraordinary leaders. Abraham Lincoln, Harry Truman, and Winston Churchill learned from their numerous failures and were strengthened and matured by these experiences.

In addition to dealing with failure, leaders must give considerable attention to other unpleasantries—handling the bad luck, the rumors, and the criticism. It is the responsibility of leaders to ensure that they maintain good communication and feedback loops relating to unfortunate events occurring within their organizations. These loops should be even better than those dealing with more normal and upbeat events. Leaders must not only actively seek out bad news, but also should understand that there will be people at various levels trying to withhold such news from them. If they are not vigilant, the information they receive will be a mere portion of the total bad news within their organizations.

No matter how perceptive, aware, and "tuned in" you may be, illegal, unethical, or unfortunate activities will occur and will go unreported. Sexual harassment, racial slurs, petty theft, drug abuse, alcoholism, and such, are the stuff of everyday life in some organizations. You must ensure that you have the procedures and the institutional support (auditors, health-care professionals, lawyers, crisis action teams, etc.) available to identify these problems and to solve them as expeditiously as possible.

You should have regular interaction with the lawyer or lawyers who work directly for you. These lawyers should be encouraged to be absolutely frank in their discussions. Decisions must be made on a regular basis as to whether an accused party needs to be counselled, given appropriate administrative punishment, or fired. Advice from lawyers is helpful concerning activities that someone is carrying out for the greater good of the organization, but that might be illegal or unethical. For example, fund-raising activities such as Bingo games, raffles, or football pools may be prohibited by state or federal law, or, in overseas areas, by local law or status of forces agreements.

The lawyer should be a very important advisor—an individual who has a high level of integrity, is energetic and "tuned in," and believes in maintaining an appropriate balance between the rights of individuals and their obligations to the organization. Listen carefully to your lawyer(s). Although you may want to overrule an attorney, this should be done only after careful analysis. An individual with substantial legal training and experience can contribute greatly to your thinking and decision-making.

Some leaders moan and groan whenever the subject of rumors, rumormongers, and the rumor mill comes up for discussion. Yet rumors can be very useful in large organizations and very helpful in a number of ways. If you stay tapped into the rumor mill, you will learn a lot. Many rumors are factual, or at least are based on some factual data. Others give you blazing flashes of insight into where problems may be within the organization. Some are wrong, and some can be dangerous, but even these can serve a good purpose, for they may alert you to an area that deserves immediate attention. Often, you can stamp out the bad rumor quickly with the decisions or facts (or both), before it does too much damage.

As I mentioned in Chapter 17, a principal of a large high school, who serves as one of my examples of an effective leader, successfully uses the rumor mill to plant ideas and information. For instance, suppose he gets the word that some of his students are planning to drive over to a rival school to assault several students for a perceived wrong of the past few days. Rather than announcing publicly his concerns and turning the issue into a confrontation between himself and some highly emotional students, he plants the word with some well-informed students that he will expel permanently anyone who goes onto the other campus and does harm to person or property. The students then know that he is tuned in, that he has laid down a very specific commitment to take strong action, and that he has the power to carry it out. They also may suspect that he has notified the other school and police may be waiting. The deterrence value of this approach can be quite powerful. The principal must, of course, be willing to follow up on his commitment, and he must be sure that the school system superintendent and his school board will support him.

Upcoming personnel actions often spark rumors that permeate an organization: X is about to be fired; Y is in line for that vacant vice president's job; Z will be the next big boss. Unfortunately, these rumors sometimes cause individuals a lot of unnecessary trauma, concern, and disappointment. Yet it is impossible to stop them from spreading. A top executive can, however, reduce the number and the impact of personnel rumors by being decisive, realistic, and, most of all, honest. A leader who procrastinates on personnel actions, or who allows a cumbersome and lengthy personnel selection and promotion system to develop, permits unnecessary time delays and encourages rumors. Leaders sometimes forget that through their indecision or procrastination, they are directly responsible for heartbreak when a rumor circulates about someone's promotion and it does not materialize. In this regard, one approach I have taken with my key staff members and subordinate leaders is as follows: "We all know that there are many important personnel activities coming up this summer. There is no way we can stop the rumors between now and the time that the big boss makes up his [her] mind. If you don't know anything and want to speculate, be my guest. However, if you are privy to inside information, please don't say anything to anybody. If the boss changes his [her] mind, some people may be terribly disappointed."

I offer one more insight concerning rumors and promotion. It stems from my personal experience when I served as commander of the F-15 fighter wing in Europe. Almost all of the previous commanders had been promoted from colonel to brigadier general while in my position. Rumors widely circulated that I would be promoted to brigadier general on the upcoming list. This did not please me. I had my dream job—the position I had wanted for many years—and had been in command only for a few months. I knew that if I was promoted, I would move on to what was, in my mind, a much less rewarding staff position. I strongly hoped that I would *not* be promoted that year, and that if promotion came, it would come after I had held command for at least two years. Yet the promotion, which did come that same year, was not only a signal of my professional success, but a signal to the wing that it was doing its job very well and had "gotten the boss promoted." Hence, I let the rumors circulate and enjoyed the collective joy that the wing felt when the boss was on the "list." It was with a heavy heart and lots of withdrawal pains that I left the wing a few months later.

Those individuals who have reached high leadership positions without one or more major setbacks in their careers are often not well-equipped to handle failure and heavy criticism. Therefore, when you are choosing individuals for leadership jobs, you may wish to look into their backgrounds to see if they have met failure and, if so, how well they handled it.

When an organization suffers a major setback, the leader should be quick to accept the blame. It is the leader's fault that the organization failed because of poor planning, poor leadership, poor organization, or the inability to anticipate potential problems. There is always a temptation to blame subordinates, fate, poor quality of the equipment, lack of guidance from above, or over-tasking. The leader should avoid these temptations. To quote the great Alabama football coach, the late Bear Bryant, "There's just three things I ever say. If anything goes bad, then I did it. If anything goes semi-good, then we did it. If anything goes really good, then you did it. That's all it takes to get people to win football games."

Fear of failure is one of the major causes of executive stress, but you should welcome an occasional setback. Failure often demonstrates that the organization is trying new approaches, setting ambitious goals, being innovative and creative, and avoiding "stand-patism" and "status-quoism." When you take your associates on an annual off-site retreat, the failures of the past year should be discussed in a very positive way. Be sure to compliment the group on the many initiatives taken. You should identify some of the failures as "heroic failures that taught us all" and those which, at a later time, may turn into grand successes. Such an approach will help everyone to bounce back from failure. By doing so, you can encourage associates to continue to reach beyond their grasp in order to accomplish great things. This is a technique that Bill Gates and Steve Ballmer use with extraordinary success at Microsoft. By encouraging their associates not to be afraid of failing, they liberate a powerfully creative work force to think and act "outside the box."

Russian military philosophy on leadership emphasizes the important point that the higher the post you occupy, the more strictly you will be judged. A leader is bound to be criticized, both fairly and unfairly, by associates within the organization, by bosses and their staffs, by competitive organizations, and by the press. A leader who becomes very thin-skinned when criticized, or who becomes defensive and somewhat paranoid, is doing a disservice to the organization. As a leader, it is important to observe your subordinate leaders and to ascertain how well they accept criticism and how willing they are to accept blame for the failures of the organization. The defensive, "blame-someone-else" individual is unlikely to succeed as a leader. By admitting failure early on, leaders often can put it behind them, take necessary corrective action, and return the organization to a higher level of performance and morale. This is one of the secrets to CNN's journalistic and business success. CNN's top leadership has established a corporate policy of acknowledging and correcting mistakes quickly.

The final element of my discussion on the "downside" of leadership involves stepping down from a position. Anyone who has ever run a complete marathon knows what it is like to hit the wall somewhere around the 20-mile mark in the 26-plus-mile race. Every muscle in the body cramps up and it is a real test of will to continue because the pain and agony are so severe. Leaders who step down from top leadership positions often experience similar problems, although the agony is mental and emotional, rather than physical. Commonly called "withdrawal pains," the stepping down from an immensely rewarding executive position can be one of the most severe emotional experiences of a person's lifetime. Since it can be so bad, it deserves a few paragraphs in this book on leadership.

For all the frustrations, long hours, after-midnight phone calls, and multiple crises, leading is, in most cases, a very uplifting and rewarding experience. Therefore, the stepping down from a leadership position, particularly one with lots of perks (executive secretaries, chauffeured cars, distinguished visitor treatment on trips, etc.) can be very traumatic indeed. It is useful to think through these withdrawal problems, in order to help you deal with the many pitfalls that may await you. One common tendency is to look back on the past leadership experience through rose-colored glasses and assume that your tenure was one of extraordinary accomplishment, high employee morale, and exceptional style and grace. The result is often a feeling that the individual who replaced you is doing a lousy job and is fouling up the marvelous institution that you created. This may cause you to be quite depressed. Since your next job may not have a very full in-box or a very heavy speaking schedule, and might lack some of the psychic rewards that your previous leadership job had, your state of depression may worsen. If this is the case, your performance in the new job will suffer. It is important to overcome these periods of depression, for your company may have great plans for you in the future, and you may have high ambitions yourself.

This is one of the many reasons that you should develop rewarding hobbies that can carry you through the quiet times of your professional career. Executives who give their entire mind, body, and soul to their work may succeed in the short run, but may fail in the long term. You must realize that one of the downsides of leadership is the trauma of withdrawal, and be prepared for it.

23

WORKING FOR
THE BIG BOSS

the trials and opportunities of the subordinate leader

Wars may be fought with weapons, but they are won by men. It is the spirit of the men who follow and of the man who leads that gains the victory.

—*George S. Patton*

All bosses have a boss.

—*Anonymous*

Whenever I conduct workshops on leadership, I almost always get a question such as, "I like many of your ideas and your rules and tools, but how do I get *my* bosses to follow your guidance?" I usually get a laugh by answering, "Have them read my book." Often, the retort to this is, "Who is going to give it to them? Not *me!*" This gets to the heart of a very important question: what is the best way to get your boss to be a better and more enlightened executive without endangering your relationship with him or her or putting your career at risk? Most executives feel that they have already demonstrated their ability to lead. They don't read management or leadership books and certainly don't think they need advice on leadership from their associates. Many bosses would be insulted if an associate gave them a book on leadership, for there would be an implied message that they needed help in this area.

So what are the answers if you are working for a leader who has deficiencies in style, substance, or both? One approach is to live with the situation and take lots of notes on how *not* to lead. When the time comes for you to be a leader, you will have a long "do not do" list. The very worst boss I ever had was extraordinarily hardworking and was the most personally ambitious individual I have ever known. But he was not very bright. He did not trust his subordinates, even though the group was of high quality. Despite valiant efforts by over a hundred professionals, he was almost always in trouble with *his* bosses. Later, when I became a boss, I was able to avoid some poor decisions because of my previous experience with this boss. It would occur to me that an action I was about to take would be something that this man might have done. I would pull up short and say to myself, "Oh no, that is *exactly* what *he* would have done. I'd better take another look." In other words, some of the best lessons an employee can learn are what *not* to do and how *not* to do it. A really bad leader can teach you hundreds of things. In fact, you can learn more from a bad leader than from a good leader, although the daily agony is painful at the time!

Another approach to dealing with weak or badly flawed bosses is to try to assist them. By making an effort to help, you will gain the respect and affection of your colleagues and you even might be able to make a difference. I have found that one of the best ways to help bosses is to approach them at a social gathering or at a sports event, when they are relaxed and open to ideas. Start the conversation with something like, "The folks on the line are really down in the dumps," or "I think we need to do something to improve the morale of our employees." If you use this kind of an opening, it is helpful to have some data that can demonstrate that there is, in fact, a morale problem of some kind. Such data might include unusually high absentee rates, an increase in the number of written complaints, negative feedback from union leaders, or a higher-than-normal rejection rate on the production line. If the boss picks up on your point, you might be able to make suggestions that will improve the situation and enhance his or her credibility. Over time, as the boss gets used to your insights, you may be able to show him or her that some past decisions were faulty and need to be reworked. I don't want to minimize the risks of trying to guide your boss, however, and some bad bosses are not only reluctant to receive advice and criticism, but are also vindictive. (Leaders who are reading this chapter might ask themselves, with as much objective introspection as they can muster, if they are receptive to criticism about their leadership.)

Another approach that may be effective is to suggest to the big boss that a subordinate leader be given an opportunity to attend a first-rate management or leadership program and to report back to the senior corporate officers on the insights that he or she gained from this experience. A better, but somewhat more risky approach is to suggest that the leader himself or herself attend one of the week-long programs at the Center for Creative Leadership at Greensboro, North Carolina, or the two-week course at the Kennedy School at Harvard University, or the four-week courses held at many of the better business schools.

If you have to work for a weak boss, it may be helpful to think in terms of categories of bosses. Working for a wimp is different than working for a "type A" boss, a power seeker, a laissez-faire individual, a mother hen, an ego tripper, or a hedonistic boss. Using commonly used phrases, let me describe various types of bosses and provide some hints on how to deal with them. In the past forty years, I have either worked for or observed at close hand each type.

Type A bosses tend to micromanage, may be workaholics, and may demand that employees work excessively long hours. They often overreact to criticism, and refuse to delegate. Subordinates should try to reason with type A bosses about unrealistic deadlines, for instance. If this doesn't work, standing up to them with firmness on a particularly unreasonable request often will get their attention and support: "I can get you an answer by the end of the day, but it will be garbage that we won't be able to use. How about giving me a week and I'll come up with something that we can all be proud of and that the big boss will like."

Power seekers love to grab pieces of the action from parts of the organization which they do not control. "Turf" is terribly important to them, and they almost never give anything up for fear that their power base may be diminished. Power seekers tend to love self-designed reorganizations that normally lead to more people, bigger budgets, and more centralization. Employees learn to treat power seekers with great care, but at times they can affect changes by demonstrating that delegation and empowerment will cause workers to work harder and more efficiently, and therefore enhance the power seeker's prestige. Subordinate leaders should explain with care that not only are the activities of the power seeker causing morale problems among the workforce, but that continuation of these activities may cause some of the more productive people to leave the firm or complain loudly to the power seeker's big boss. Leaders on "power trips" tend to be personally insecure, and sometimes subordinates can play on these insecurities to help the power seekers curb their dysfunctional proclivities.

Wimpy bosses tend to be non-decisive and are afraid to take strong action in any direction. Their philosophy of leadership seems to be "no runs, no hits, and no errors." For example, a wimpy boss would prefer to limp along with a weak associate, rather than to fire that individual. As a subordinate associate, you can help a wimpy boss by making decisions for him or her and keeping him or her informed of the decisions that you have already made. If things go wrong, you will have to take the blame. You may not get credit for the successes, but at least the organization will not be paralyzed. One technique that I have used with non-decisive bosses is to send them notes informing them about an action I was about to take, and suggesting that if I did not hear from them within a week, I would press on. I indicated that I was willing to take full responsibility for my action, in order to ease their minds. This is the "silence means consent" approach to making things happen.

Laissez-faire bosses are usually good ones for whom to work, in that they leave you alone and allow you to make decisions on your own. However, such a boss can become too far removed from the action. If this occurs, try to keep him or her informed, regarding important issues, so that you don't stray significantly from the boss's views on these issues. You are likely to have the opportunity to shape a laissez-faire boss's views and the policy of the organization. Just be sure to do so responsibly, honestly, and carefully.

Country club bosses are so interested in their golf games, the next social event, or the next trip to the Bahamas that they get more and more out-of-touch with what is going on. Unlike a laissez-faire boss, who is interested but believes in delegation and empowerment, the country club boss simply has lost interest and may not even be willing to help you when you ask for assistance. It may be useful to keep an informal association with the boss at the next level up or, if your boss is the president of the organization, to establish contact with key members of the Board of Directors, so that you can receive help and support.

Captured-by-the-staff bosses normally have a large and talented staff that successfully steers the boss around. This can be quite satisfying for the staff, especially if the boss is willing to take decisions and to stick with them. However, this situation can be very frustrating to subordinate leaders in the plants, regional offices, and field activity centers, particularly when the leader makes poor decisions based on faulty or biased staff advice. If you run facilities that are geographically removed from the corporate offices, first attempt to pursue issues through the staff, in hopes of getting staff support for your ideas or initiatives. If this course is not successful, then try to get the boss to meet with you on a regular basis at a place where the staff is not present, so that you can lay out your concerns frankly and forthrightly with the boss. Finally, the direct approach can be helpful in certain circumstances: "We all admire you out here in the field, but we are having a tough time with your staff." Or perhaps, "You have a great staff, but they have lost track with the real world out here."

Big ego bosses only want to hear that what they have done is right. These bosses never want to be challenged about their judgment, wisdom, or decisions. They become defensive when criticized, and tend to contradict and threaten anyone who raises the criticism. If something good happens, the boss is the cause; if something bad happens, it is always someone else's fault. Avoid direct criticism of this boss. By being very diplomatic, however, a subordinate can plant ideas into the boss's mind that the boss will think are his or her own. When the boss takes full credit for your idea or for the idea of one of your associates, do not challenge the point, but be sure to give yourself some credit or to thank and reward the associate yourself.

Mother hen bosses give too much specific guidance on even the most routine matters. These bosses treat associates as if they were grammar school children or people of low intelligence. If your superior is a mother hen boss, ask for a private session and diplomatically explain that you are fully capable of doing these routine tasks with little or no guidance. If this approach is not feasible, find ways to keep so busy that you do not have time to meet with the boss for long guidance sessions. A third approach is to suggest to the boss that he or she handle certain issues, so you can concentrate your efforts on other issues. Some mother hen bosses feel guilty if they are not busy all the time, and this third approach may help keep them from bothering you with too much advice.

The *retired-in-place boss* is approaching the end of his or her career and no longer has much energy or interest in trying to do anything new, in communicating with associates, or in handling customers' issues. These bosses often can be recognized by the regular use of the statement, "Let's go back to the good old ways of doing things." Many of these bosses want to enjoy the fruits of their years of hard work by taking their last year or two off from any productive involvement in the leadership of the organization. Try to see this as an opportunity to take initiatives on your own. If your ideas require the boss to do little or no work, he or she very well may accept them. Another approach is to appeal to the boss in terms of establishing a legacy. Many bosses who are inclined to goof off will be motivated by a subtle appeal to their egos—a "we would like to see you retire on a high note" argument. Another useful approach is to try to get the boss to do a lot of traveling the last year. This should allow you and your fellow associates to take some action while the boss is gone.

Too often, subordinates take a hands-off approach to poor leadership at the top. If the American economic, political, and military systems are going to thrive in the next century, it is incumbent upon associates and executives alike to take steps to improve the leadership of this nation's companies, government agencies, and nonprofit institutions.

Although this brief chapter was written largely for subordinate associates, there is considerable utility here for the leader. If you perceive that associates are doing some of the things suggested above, it may be that *you* are the source of some of the problems your organization is experiencing. Few leaders are as good as they think they are, and listening for signals is an important part of the leadership equation.

Followership and leadership are closely linked. Leaders need good followers; followers need good leaders; and both groups need the positive interaction and chemistry between them if the institution, organization, or company is to thrive. Subordinate associates should remember that no executive wants to fail, that no leader wants to be labeled a wimp, a geek, or an autocrat. Those who understand that leadership brings out either the very best or the very worst in an individual, and who are willing to help the leader reach for the best, can be marvelous contributors to excellence and good morale.

You learn a great deal from observing leaders, both good and bad. By seeking and obtaining as many opportunities to exercise leadership as the delegation, empowerment, or apathy of the boss will allow, you can prepare yourself for the great challenges and opportunities that lie ahead. A regular reading program, periodic attendance at executive development seminars, and keeping a file of good quotations, humorous stories, and jokes can help. In addition, actively seek out leadership opportunities in the local community, in church or temple, and in professional associations and clubs. Finally, as you work your way up the corporate or institutional hierarchy, keep in mind that when you become the leader, large numbers of people will be relying on you to be the very best that you can be.

24

WRAPPING IT UP
putting it all together

American organizations have been over managed and under led.
— *Warren Bennis*

The greatest problem facing America may be the short supply of "gifted generalists."

— *Harlan Cleveland*

This book has been designed to give you practical thoughts on how to run an organization. Although Appendix A provides a number of checklists, it is important to emphasize that complete reliance on "checklist" or "cookbook" leadership can be a mistake. Anyone who runs an organization but cannot adapt to the day-to-day situations not contained in checklists is doomed to fail as an enlightened leader. Therefore, you should accept the ideas, insights, and checklists that are provided with a certain amount of skepticism. Much that happens in any organization is truly unique; however, the lessons of others may be helpful as you face current challenges.

As a leader, it is important for you to do your own thinking, to read widely, and to talk with and listen to others inside and outside your organization. Leaders should never rely on one or two key associates or assistants to do their thinking for them. If they do so, in a very real sense, they are no longer leaders.

Throughout this text, I have tried to emphasize that the leader's task of decision-making is a complicated one. Before you make a decision for your organization, it is useful to ask questions: "Who is going to be mad? How mad?"; "Who is going to be happy? How happy?" This insight, from Paul Appleby, is useful, for it highlights the need to anticipate the reactions of associates and others who may be affected by your decisions. Anticipating reactions should not paralyze you, but considering them will help you to frame the right questions before you make those leadership decisions. Your decisions will affect not only you, but many others. This is a profound and often invigorating aspect of leadership.

Good leaders are focused people who are willing to make tough decisions. James Stockdale, who has written so powerfully about leadership, has good advice for all of us. He believes that individuals who are not willing to discipline people, who are unwilling to remove incompetents, and who crave to be loved tend to be poor leaders.

It is vitally important that, as a leader, you do not let the urgent issues force out the important ones in your day-to-day schedule. Furthermore, spend your talents lavishly, rather than hoard them. Leadership should be a giving, not a taking, experience. Your attitude is important because the posture assumed in daily activities can have a great impact on the morale of the organization. If a leader is a negative person, it is likely that employees will adopt a negative disposition. On the other hand, if a leader is cheerful, the pleasantness will spread throughout the organization. People want to feel good about themselves, their bosses, their organization, and what they are doing.

Many leaders fail to fully exploit the various means available to motivate their people to higher levels of commitment, performance excellence, and integrity. You periodically should take a hard look (at least annually) at the various formal and informal incentive programs. Is the annual bonus system robust enough? Is it fair? Is it perceived as being fair by employees at all levels? How effective are various Employees of the Month, Manager of the Year, Salesperson of the Quarter programs? Are the right people being selected and are the awards being properly publicized? Do the recipients get monetary awards, time off, or certificates? Are these awards the ones that your employees really want, or are there others that would have more impact? Don't forget to develop awards that reward the average worker for above-average work. The "most improved" kinds of awards are very useful motivators to the folks at lower levels who otherwise might never be singled out for recognition.

Many suggestion and "new ideas" programs focus on only one part of the enterprise and neglect other areas. Awards for the design of the better wrench to improve assembly line or maintenance efficiency are fine and should be continued. However, the person who comes up with the next new concept or strategy may impact on the bottom line much more significantly. Associates should not only be rewarded for the great new concept; they should also be motivated to continue to think about conceptual innovation.

There is lots of empirical evidence showing that positive expectations lead to positive results. This "Pygmalion effect" should serve as a beacon of truth and inspiration for all leaders. Tell people that they are outstanding, that they can accomplish a great deal and, in most cases, they will meet or exceed your expectations.

Some leaders, however, go overboard and place unrealistic demands of perfection on their associates. One of my heroes, Medal of Honor winner Jack Jacobs, gave me a wonderful set of insights about bosses. He pointed out to me that "a leader of a large organization may often have to accept rotten circumstances in order to make overall progress. The high-level leader who will accept nothing less than the perfection that can be achieved only at great cost will lose everything. This is not to say that standards must be low; on the contrary, it is at the highest levels that high standards originate. But the leader has to have the kind of long-range vision that will overlook short-term setbacks." If you are a leader or potential leader of a large organization, you must understand this truism: "The perfect can be the enemy of the good." A leader crosses an important milestone when signing that first imperfect, but wholly adequate staff paper without personally editing or changing it.

Leadership functions must be shared with "lieutenants." The organization will become healthier as you create more centers of leadership within it. If you have a deputy, take particular care in nurturing your relationship with him or her. A deputy leader must be given authority to make decisions in your absence, and you must enthusiastically support those decisions. The deputy should be included in all substantive meetings, discussions, and decisions, so that the entire institution understands that he or she has authority, responsibility, and credibility.

If your role as leader was preceded by experiences limited to a specialized area, whether it be marketing, personnel, logistics, engineering, operations, or any other, you must take steps to grow beyond that specialized field. A true leader will always be fundamentally challenged, rather than repelled, by complexity. A good leader focuses primarily on opportunities, not on problems; he or she is a generalist. If you are in the position to select individuals for leadership positions, choose individuals who have the capacity to grow and to become gifted generalists.

If the leader is to ensure organizational creativity and innovation, there must be tolerance for the creative fanatic who, in many cases, is the force behind important changes. Organizations often suppress new ideas, new opinions, and new alternatives. Leaders must fight against the bureaucratic tendencies to create watered-down compromises that are often less-than-desirable solutions. There is a sign on a rural road in upstate New York that says, "Choose your rut carefully; you will be in it for the next 25 miles." A good leader identifies the "ruts" within an organization and makes sure that individuals or groups of individuals do not stay in these "ruts" for the next twenty-five weeks, twenty-five months, or twenty-five years.

Leaders must be capable of operating simultaneously at the tactical, operational, and strategic levels. The higher leaders move up in their organizations, the more they must think and act strategically. Senior leaders should never make tactical decisions without first considering the strategic implications of the decision.

In every organization, there are many people who are not pulling their share of the load because of their own incompetencies, laziness, poor attitudes, psychological difficulties, bad habits, or family problems. Part of your role as leader is to deal with these people and to motivate them, counsel them, or, as a last resort, remove them. One of the frustrating things about dealing with large organizations is the difficulty in removing incompetent individuals. You must be very aggressive in this regard; although it might take a great amount of time and effort to deal with incompetents, the effectiveness and morale of the organization depends upon maintaining high standards of competence and integrity. If a leader is not willing to establish, maintain, and enforce those standards, the organization will suffer.

I purposefully have not written a chapter on women or on racial or ethnic minorities in leadership positions because it is my strong belief that the art of leadership is not something that is unique to any one group of people. However, I do feel that there are different cultural and historical environments that impact significantly on the rules of leadership in various parts of the world. For example, leaders in China are very different from leaders in the United States. I also feel that leadership requirements vary considerably in different historical settings; leadership in the historical context of France's Napoleonic era was different than it is in the France of today, which now enjoys a rich democratic tradition that has been in place for more than a century.

Within the democratic tradition of Western nations, the ground rules are quite similar, whether the organization is being led by a woman, an Asian, a Black, a Latino, or another member of a minority group. Dynamic and effective female leaders have shown that women do superbly in leadership positions and generally follow the ground rules for the cultural environment in which they operate. Examples are: Margaret Thatcher of Great Britain; Gro Brutland of Norway; and Jeane Kirkpatrick, Madeleine Albright, and Elizabeth Dole of the United States. The same can be said for African-Americans, Asian-Americans, Latinos, and other minority groups in America.

Those who make a strong differentiation between men and women or between racial groups in leadership roles tend to do so based on a few personal experiences, rather than upon an examination of the large amount of empirical data that is now available. The real question is not whether women or people from minority groups can be great leaders, for it has already been proven that they can. Instead, it involves how women and minorities can get the jobs that will lead to prominent leadership posts. For readers who are interested in the topic of women in leadership positions, I recommend Sally Helgesen's *The Female Advantage: Women's Ways of Leadership*, and Carol Gilligan's *In a Different Voice*.

As I draw this short book to a close, I would like to emphasize the importance of metaphors and leverage. There are many marvelous metaphors that can help people understand the leadership mindset. My favorite one relates to the choreographer. First, she designs the dance. Then she gets on the stage with the dancers and walks them through the movements. Next, she plays the music and slowly works the dancers through the specifics and the nuances of the dance. At some point, she takes a very important step—she climbs up to the balcony and views the dance from a distance. Without interruption, the full dance number is performed. Like the choreographer, all leaders need to climb up on their "balconies" and take a strategic view of what they are doing, how they are spending their time, and how well they are making and carrying out their decisions. All leaders need to carve out a two-hour period each month to become strategic and climb up to their "balconies."

Another great metaphor for the leader is that of a mountain climber who relies on the belayer. As part of the superb Kellogg National Leadership Program (see Appendix D, page 275), I spent a week in Leadville with Colorado Outward Bound. All participants had to climb a 150-foot vertical cliff. Before we started our climb, we put on helmets and harnesses. Ropes were tossed down from the top of the cliff. Each climber tied one end of the safety rope to his or her harness. On the top of the cliff was a person who held the other end and served as a belayer. This person, who was tied to a tree at the top of the cliff, had an important job. As I slowly climbed (I was not permitted to use the safety rope during the climb), the belayer was to keep the rope reasonably taut. If I fell, the rope was supposed to catch me. When I started my climb, I knew that there was a belayer up top, but I didn't know if it was someone who could bench-press 400 pounds or if it was someone who had little physical strength. I had to trust a person who had been trained to be a belayer within the previous few minutes. During that climb, I had to be willing to be both trusting and vulnerable—two of the most important qualities for leaders to develop.

Let me switch gears and discuss how the best leaders who I've observed use leverage to maximize their abilities to serve the mission and their people. Just as a workman can use a long bar as a fulcrum to lift a very heavy weight, leaders can use leverage to accomplish great things. Using carefully developed skills, top leaders can leverage their braintrust, their technology, their skills, and their time. Many have a very robust braintrust of people whom they can call on for advice, solace, and strategic perspective. Modern leaders deftly use technology such as computers, spelling checkers, voice recognition software, and the internet. Many are speed readers and use dictation well; they employ these skills to absorb a great deal of information and, in turn, to get information out quickly and efficiently. Finally, all of these outstanding leaders discipline their daily schedules, their meetings, and their telephone use, in order to maximize their very valuable time. Whereas integrity is the most vital quality of leadership, and listening is the most vital skill, leverage is the most crucial talent of the twenty-first century leader.

Leadership is not keeping your boss happy; avoiding trouble; accumulating power, perks, and privileges; staying really busy; or getting to the bottom of your in-box. Leadership is serving your people, serving the mission, giving power away, and raising the level of dignity and integrity in your organization. There is no activity in human endeavor that is more fascinating, more challenging, and more rewarding than leading an organization with an important mission. People who are willing to grow, learn, listen, acknowledge mistakes, teach subordinate associates, set goals, and maintain high standards are leaders who can help lift an organization to new heights. Tom Cronin challenges each of us when he suggests that leaders have those indispensable qualities of contagious self-confidence, unwarranted optimism, and incurable idealism that allow them to attract and mobilize others to undertake tasks these people never dreamed they could undertake. This is the true role of the leader.

APPENDIX A
checklists and guidelines for the busy leader

> *Whatever advice you give, be short.*
> —*Horace*

The following checklists are provided to help you accomplish several of the important tasks that confront you, as a leader. They serve two basic purposes: they help to ensure that a pressing task is accomplished in an effective manner; and they reduce the chance that a vital step or element will be left out. These checklists are not substitutes for judgment, but they can trigger the thinking process and make the task at hand somewhat easier. Also included within this section are some basic rules of thumb, appropriate and inappropriate phrases, helpful thoughts, and quick reminders.

I am especially appreciative to the military, for teaching me the value of checklists. More recently, Sam Deep and Lyle Sussman have given me many valuable insights on how to construct and use checklists. Deep and Sussman have written a number of books that provide excellent checklists for many occasions. (See Appendix E, page 280.)

This appendix contains:
1. Transition Checklist
2. Meeting Checklist
3. Decision-Making Checklist
4. Hiring Checklist

5. Firing Checklist
6. Communications Checklist
7. Performance Counseling Checklist
8. Pet Peeve Checklist
9. Integrity Checklist
10. Rules for Brainstorming
11. Leadership Skills Checklist
12. Introspection Checklist
13. Phrases to Avoid Checklist
14. Planning Checklist
15. Thank You Checklist
16. Crisis Leadership Checklist
17. Press Conference and Media Interview Checklist
18. Risk-Taking Checklist
19. Divestiture Checklist
20. Change Leadership Checklist
21. Promotion Board Checklist
22. Congressional Visit Checklist
23. Congressional Testimony Checklist
24. Rules of Thumb for Congressional Testimony
25. Telltale Phrases to Listen For
26. Cynical Expressions to Listen For
27. Useful Short Phrases for Leaders
28. Useful Phrases for Confident Associates
29. Thoughts for All Seasons
30. Blazing Flashes of the Obvious

---

1. Transition Checklist

As soon as you have been selected to fill a leadership position, your research must begin. It is crucial that you have a full grasp of your organization's agenda, history, strengths, weaknesses, potential, strategies, and staff. The following questions are useful to ask as you assume your new role. They are also helpful questions to answer if you are stepping down and handing your tasks over to a new leader.

- ❐ What is the organization's mission?
- ❐ In order to accomplish that mission, what are the organization's:
  —goals?
  —priorities?
  —plans?
  —programs?
  —budgets?
- ❐ What is the size and structure of the organization?
- ❐ Who is my boss?
  —what is his or her leadership/management style?
  —how does he or she communicate with me?
  —what does he or she expect of me and when?
  —what are his or her pet peeves?
- ❐ What means of communication will I have?
  —staff meetings?
  —formal and informal workshops?
  —social gatherings?
  —newspaper/newsletter?
  —radio?
  —television?
- ❐ Who reports directly to me?
  —how many?
  —why?
  —why not others?

❐ Which organizations, corporate staff offices, and individuals should I visit?
  —in what order?
  —how often (for subsequent visits)?

❐ Am I responsible for geographically separated units?
  —do they report directly/indirectly to me?

❐ What are the major logistics problems?

❐ Where are the personnel strengths, shortages, and weaknesses?

❐ What are the standards of integrity?
  —have there been recent violations of these standards?
  —how frequent are these violations?
  —what was the outcome of each violation?

❐ What are the standards of performance?
  —how are they measured?
  —what are the results of recent:
    —outside inspections?
    —self-inspections?
    —audits?

❐ What documents should I read?
  —in what order?
  —is there an annual organizational history? if not, why not?
  —is there a book of standard operating procedures; organizational regulations?
  —is there a published strategic plan? if not, why not?

❐ What skeletons are in what closets?
  —organizational skeletons?
  —personal skeletons?

❐ What are the toughest problems and issues I should expect to face during the first few months?

❐ Who are the key informal leaders?

❐ What is the condition of the industrial plant, buildings, unit equipment, etc.?

❐ How often do the top leaders and their immediate subordinates go to "off-site" workshops together?

❐ Did the previous leader have a philosophy letter?
—what should I include in my philosophy letter?

2. Meeting Checklist

This checklist will be helpful to the executive, his or her immediate staff, and to any corporate officer, factory manager, or division chief who is responsible for chairing meetings. Its purpose
is to improve the effectiveness of the meeting environment, thus
reducing the length and the frustrations of undisciplined meetings.

- ❏ What is the purpose of the meeting? What is the agenda?
- ❏ Who will be in attendance?
    - —have invitations been sent to all the corporate divi-
      sions, regional offices, international bureaus, factories,
      sales offices, etc.?
    - —is a lawyer in attendance, if appropriate?
    - —is a public affairs person in attendance, if appropriate?
- ❏ If key players cannot attend, can they be hooked up
  through a conference call, a teleconference system, or some
  other means?
- ❏ Do I intend to run the meeting myself or to allow someone
  else to chair the meeting?
- ❏ Do I have an overall policy on length of meetings, number
  of presentations, and length of presentations?
    - —in this meeting, do I intend to hold to these con-
      straints?
    - —if not, do I intend to announce my position at the start
      of the meeting?
- ❏ How much time is allocated for the meeting?
    - —what is the start time and the end time?
    - —have I announced the start and end times of the meet-
      ing ahead of time?
    - —do any key players have to leave early? if so, who?
      should the agenda be adjusted accordingly?
- ❏ Are there presentations to be made?
    - —if so, by whom?

—are there time limits placed on each presentation?

—will there be enough time for adequate discussion?

☐ What is my plan for keeping the meeting on track?

☐ What is my meeting strategy?
  —who are the main antagonists?
  —is compromise possible?
  —is compromise wise? will it lead to a watered-down solution?

☐ Will decisions be made during the meeting?
  —if so, will I announce them at the end?
  —if not, should I announce when and how the decisions will be made?

☐ Who will be responsible for the implementation of the decisions?

☐ Who will be the recorder for the meeting?
  —will there be minutes?
  —will action items be committed to writing after the meeting?

☐ Will additional meetings be needed?
  —should these meetings be announced prior to the end of this meeting?
  —if not, will I announce that this is the final meeting on the subject?

3. Decision-Making Checklist

Before finalizing each decision, use this checklist to improve the quality of the decision and to prevent avoidable mistakes.

- ❏ Has the coordination been completed?

- ❏ Have all key line and staff agencies had the opportunity to comment, criticize, or express their nonconcurrence on the options and recommendations?

- ❏ Do I have the authority to make this decision? If not, who does?

- ❏ Is this the right time to decide?

- ❏ Would postponing the decision help or hurt the mission of the organization?

- ❏ Does the decision conform to our strategic plan?

- ❏ Is the decision faithful to my goals and priorities?

- ❏ If I am about ready to launch off in a new direction, do I need to change our strategic plan, our goals, or our priorities?

- ❏ Is the decision consistent with my previous decisions?

- ❏ What will be the general reaction throughout my organization?
    —will it help or hurt morale?
    —will it undermine my legitimacy as the leader?
    —will it significantly enhance output or mission accomplishment?

- ❏ Has informal coordination with outside organizations already taken place?
    —if not, should I telephone some key people to make sure that my decision doesn't receive too much negative reaction and criticism?

- ❏ How should this decision be announced?

—at a press conference?
—at a staff meeting?
—by a decision letter?
—by telephone calls to superiors and key subordinate associates?

❒ Does the statement announcing the decision include a complete rationale for the decision?

❒ Have I carefully weighed the seven decision checks? (See Chapter 8.)
—the sanity check
—the dignity check
—the systems check
—the *60 Minutes, CNN,* or *Washington Post* check
—the safety check
—the strategy check
—the integrity check

---
4. Hiring Checklist

When you are hiring someone for a key position, holding a personal interview will allow you to get a "feel" for the candidate and for the "chemistry" between the two of you. If a face-to-face interview is not possible, an interview by telephone may be an acceptable substitute. Asking the following questions will yield responses that will reveal a lot about the interviewee.

- ❑ Do you want the job? Why?

- ❑ What talents, qualities, and strengths can you bring to this job?

- ❑ What are your weaknesses?

- ❑ What experience do you have with:
  —operations?
  —planning?
  —finance/marketing?
  —research and development?
  —personnel?
  —computer systems?

- ❑ How many people have you led or supervised in your career?

- ❑ What is your leadership/management style?

- ❑ If I asked one of your associates to describe you and your leadership style, what would be the response?

- ❑ If you are not selected, whom would you recommend for this job?

- ❑ Have you ever fired anyone?

- ❑ Have you ever been fired?

- ❑ Have you had any setbacks in your career?
  —if so, what were the most significant lessons learned from the setbacks?
  —what organizational setbacks have you observed first hand?

❐ What is the toughest problem that you have faced in your professional career?
   —how did you handle it?

❐ What are your long-term personal goals?

❐ For how long would you like to hold this job?

❐ Do you expect to be promoted quickly?

❐ Are there any "skeletons in your closets?"

❐ What are the best books that you have read in the last few years?
   —what insights did they provide you?

❐ In your present organization, who do you admire the most and why?

❐ What are the standards of integrity in your present organization?

❐ Are you considering any other positions?

❐ If I select you for this job, will you take it as your first choice over the other positions that you are considering?

❐ What questions have I failed to ask you?

❐ What questions do you have for me?

5. Firing Checklist

The difficult duty of firing an associate can be made somewhat easier if it is accomplished systematically. It is best that you maintain a sense of concern and empathy while, at the same time, sticking with the decision to remove the individual. During the session, the associate should be given adequate time to vent displeasure or disagreement with the decision. You can gain useful insights about problems within the organization through passive listening. Remain sure-footed and focused. Carefully prepare by following the below-listed guidelines.

❏ Outline reasons for the decision:
    —loss of confidence in employee's abilities.
    —lack of adequate competence:
        —as a supervisor/leader/manager.
        —as a writer.
        —as a teacher.
    —lack of ability to meet deadlines.
    —lack of integrity.
    —poor attitude.
    —chronic absenteeism.
    —inability to get along with boss/peers/subordinates.
    —inability to keep up with rapidly changing technology.
    —inability to establish warm relationships with customers.

❏ Ask what he or she might want to do next and how I can help.

❏ Ask what lessons can be drawn from this setback.

❏ Ask if there are any things about which I may not be aware, concerning the organization.

❏ Offer professional assistance (for example, a psychiatrist, a financial advisor, a lawyer, or an outplacement service), if appropriate.

❐ Explain what kind of effectiveness report he or she can expect, and to what extent, if any, I am willing to give references to prospective employers.

6. Communications Checklist

Many leaders fail to use fully the means of communication that are, or can be made, available to them. Use this checklist to ensure that opportunities are not missed.

❏ Is there an organization newspaper?
   —how often is it published?
   —what is its quality?
   —how wide is the readership?
   —is there a space reserved for the leader's weekly / monthly column?
   —what percentage of the recipients of the newspaper actually reads the leader's column?
   —is there a feedback channel?
      —letters to the editor?
      —an action line?

❏ Do I have regular access to:
   —radio?
   —television?
   —closed-circuit television?
   —video-conferencing?

❏ Is there a public affairs office?
   —if so, does the director report directly to me? If not, why not?
   —what are the director's ideas on how best to communicate with the people?

❏ Is electronic mail used throughout the organization? if not, why not?
   —do associates have direct access to me via e-mail?
   —do I answer my e-mail promptly?

❏ Are there regular staff meetings?
   —are minutes taken, published, and circulated?
   —do participants feel free to raise issues?

❏ Are there work-unit meetings?

☐ Are subordinate organizations being publicly praised and thanked?
   —in what ways and through what means?

☐ Is there a movie or videotape that explains the organization to new people, visitors, guests, families, community leaders, the media, etc.? If not, why not?

☐ Do I take advantage of the informal means of communication, taking coffee breaks with associates, participating in bowling leagues or golf tournaments, and attending company social and sporting events?

7. Performance Counselling Checklist

This checklist can be a helpful guide when you have one-on-one counselling sessions with your associates. Any checklist used in this regard should be committed to memory, so that the meeting does not become too formal or structured. Prior to your semiannual series of one-on-one sessions, you may wish to circulate a memo of questions along the general lines of this checklist, to give your associates an idea of the topics that will be discussed. Thus, they will be better prepared and more at ease.

- ❏ What aspects of this organization do you like the most?

- ❏ What issues around here concern you the most?

- ❏ What are your ideas for improving this organization?

- ❏ In your judgment, who are the most innovative, helpful, and cooperative people in this organization?

- ❏ What personal goals have you set for yourself while you are here?

- ❏ Where and to what job would you like to go next?
  —why?
  —when?

- ❏ What do you think your chances are for promotion to the next rank or position, and in what time frame?

- ❏ What do you consider to be your most significant weaknesses?

- ❏ What self-improvement programs do you have underway?

- ❏ What three things cause you to waste your time the most?

- ❏ Do I do anything that wastes your time?

- ❏ What bothers you the most about my decisions and my leadership style?

- ❏ Do I do things that embarrass you?
  —if so, what things?

❏ What kind of personal development program does your department have for minority groups?
  —how successful is it?

❏ What goals have you established for your organization?

❏ Please evaluate the performance of the organization, unit, or group that you have led over the past year [or in the period since the last one-on-one session], outlining the high and low points of the period.

❏ What organizations, factories, programs, staff functions, branch or regional offices, etc. should we divest?
  —on what kind of schedule—now, next year, five years from now, etc.?

8. Pet Peeve Checklist

When you begin serving in a new leadership position, and periodically thereafter, review your pet peeves or "hang-ups" and articulate them to your associates. Since a pet peeve checklist is a personal statement on your biases, concerns, and idiosyncrasies, you really must prepare your own. The following checklist is provided for illustrative purposes and should be used only as a very general guide.

- ❐ Low levels of integrity.
- ❐ Careerism/hyperambition.
- ❐ Authoritarianism.
- ❐ Lack of style.
- ❐ Missing deadlines.
- ❐ Retirement on the job.
- ❐ Parochialism.
- ❐ Being used.
- ❐ Rumormongering.
- ❐ Dilettantism or superficiality.
- ❐ Not telling the full story.
- ❐ Vindictiveness.

9. Integrity Checklist

Within an organization, there are certain areas and processes that especially challenge integrity. It is important for you, as leader, to check periodically the following systems and procedures, in order to ensure that high standards of integrity are being maintained.

- ❏ Inspection system.
- ❏ Training system.
- ❏ Management control system.
- ❏ Reporting system.
- ❏ Testing system.
- ❏ Congressional testimony.
- ❏ Submission of programs and budgets.
- ❏ Training competitions.
- ❏ Records within the personnel system.
- ❏ Recognition/award system.
- ❏ Bonus system.
- ❏ Expense accounts.
- ❏ Hiring practices.
- ❏ Equal opportunity programs.
- ❏ Prerequisites.
- ❏ Soliciting of members for groups.
- ❏ Soliciting of monetary contributions.
- ❏ Inventory control and fund control in quasi-official clubs or organizations.
- ❏ Covert operations (where applicable).

10. Rules for Brainstorming

Leadership in the twenty-first century involves much more than managing resources and leading people. It encompasses the promotion and utilization of creativity and innovation. A marvelous way to encourage and enhance the creativity process is the use of regular and disciplined brainstorming. To set up an oral brainstorming session, pick from eight to twelve bright people, sit them in a circle, and state the problem, issue, or plan about which you are going to brainstorm. Start the process by asking someone to present an idea. Do not discuss the idea, but go immediately to the next person in the circle. Continue to go around the room until every idea has been presented. *Then, and only then, is discussion permitted.*

Keep in mind that electronic brainstorming is a dynamic alternative to oral brainstorming.

The general rules for oral brainstorming are:

❒ No idea is a bad idea.

❒ The wilder the idea, the better.

❒ Strive for quantity, not quality of ideas.

❒ Have an assigned recorder write down every idea.

❒ Stamp out "killer phrases" early. (Killer phrases suppress creativity, especially among new and/or shy associates. See *Killer Phrases*, below.)

❒ Draw out the introverts by calling upon them during the discussion period.

❒ Dismiss the group and pull out the best of the ideas.

Killer Phrases:

❒ "A good idea, but . . ."   ❒ "It's all right in theory, but . . ."

❒ "It's against company   ❒ "Be practical."
   policy."   ❒ "It costs too much."

❏ "It needs more study."   ❏ "That's not our problem."

❏ "Get real!"   ❏ "The boss won't buy it."

❏ "You've gotta be kidding!"   ❏ "Let's form a committee."

❏ "It's not in the budget."   ❏ "We tried that before."

❏ "It's not part of our job."   ❏ "It will never work."

The big advantages of brainstorming are:

❏ Some fresh ideas will surface.

❏ It helps you find the very best thinkers, innovators, and conceptualizers.

❏ It lets your people know that you are open to innovation.

❏ It's a good team-building exercise.

11. Leadership Skills Checklist

The enhancement of leadership skills will improve your effectiveness, your time management, and your quality of life. I suggest that you glance over this checklist at least once every six months.

❏ What are my major weaknesses as a leader?
   —what am I doing to improve these weak areas?

❏ Is my schedule adequately arranged?
   —have I provided definitive scheduling guidelines to my secretary [assistant]?
   —does my daily schedule assign more than one event per hour? am I over-scheduled?
   —do I have time to think, to write, to plan, to be introspective?

❏ Concerning my yearly calendar, when do I plan to have my off-site seminar?
   —when do I plan to schedule my one-on-one sessions with key associates?
   —on what schedule do I plan to visit the geographically separated field organizations?
   —what is my vacation schedule?

❏ By what means do new ideas bubble up to the top in my organization?

❏ How many new ideas have been implemented in the past year?

❏ Am I perceived as:
   —out of touch?
   —past my prime?
   —authoritarian?
   —non-decisive?
   —a captive of my staff?
   —arrogant?
   —overly intense?

—biased?
—self-righteous?
—lazy?
—a micromanager?
—an alcoholic?
—lacking in style?
—preoccupied?
—aloof?

❐ Who in the organization is totally frank with me?
  —what are my associates saying about me over a cup of coffee or at the bar?
  —which associates are sycophants—bootlickers or apple polishers?

❐ Am I skilled in giving dictation:
  —to my secretary?
  —to a dictaphone?
  —to voice recognition software in my computer?

❐ Am I a speed reader? If not, do I plan to take a course in speed reading soon?

❐ Am I taking full advantage of available avenues of communication?
  —an organizational newspaper, magazine, or newsletter?
  —television and/or radio?
  —audiotapes and/or videotapes?
  —electronic mail?
  —staff and work-unit meetings?
  —social events?

❐ When was the last time I rewrote my philosophy letter?

❐ What legacy do I wish to leave behind me?

❐ Who is capable of replacing me?

12. Introspection Checklist

Introspection is an important part of leadership. Leaders who know who they are, who recognize and use their strengths while understanding and compensating for their weaknesses, have a tremendous advantage. They perform much better than leaders who cannot or do not analyze and evaluate themselves. The following checklist provides a framework for objective introspection.

- ❐ Do I plan my weekly and monthly schedules carefully?
  —do I follow them fairly closely?

- ❐ Does my secretary [assistant] help to maintain my schedule?

- ❐ Have I established organizational priorities?
  —do my associates and I consistently stick to these priorities?

- ❐ How reliable am I?
  —how many meetings, speeches, trips, social engagements, professional commitments, etc. have I cancelled during the last month?

- ❐ Who tells me all of the news—good and bad?

- ❐ How long are my meetings?

- ❐ How well do I listen? When I interact with others, do I spend at least 75 percent of my time listening?

- ❐ What is my body language saying?

- ❐ Do my associates:
  —fear me?
  —distrust me?
  —like me?
  —love me?
  —respect me?

- ❐ How courteous am I?

- ❐ Do I enjoy my job?
- ❐ Am I considered a communicator?
- ❐ Am I a delegator?
- ❐ Am I considered a disciplinarian?
- ❐ Am I flexible?
- ❐ Am I "tuned in" or "out of touch"?
- ❐ Am I decisive or am I a "decision ducker"?
- ❐ Do I maintain physical and intellectual fitness?
- ❐ Am I a deflector of pressure from above, or a magnifier of that pressure?
- ❐ Am I an optimist or a pessimist?
- ❐ Am I secure or insecure?
- ❐ Am I intense or am I relaxed?
- ❐ Am I ambitious?
- ❐ What is my integrity level?
- ❐ What are my ethics and values?
- ❐ Am I a nondrinker, a drinker, or an alcoholic?
- ❐ Am I a writer?
- ❐ How "conceptual" am I?
- ❐ Do I promote diversity?

---

13. Phrases to Avoid Checklist

Leaders must choose their words carefully. It is easy to say counterproductive things out of haste or emotion. Although some statements work well within small organizations, many are not appropriate for larger environments. Here are a few commonly used phrases that I have found, in my experience, just don't work well for the executives.

☐ *"Make it happen now."*
This statement often leads to cutting corners and the violation of personal or organizational integrity. Also, it often results in decisions that are not well-coordinated, thoughtful, or in accordance with established priorities.

☐ *"I don't care how you get it done, just do it."*
Much like the previous phrase, this is an invitation to your employees to take shortcuts, to be dishonest, or to act illegally. Many leaders learn the hard way that this can be an avenue to disaster.

☐ *"I don't get mad—I get even."*
The above phrase lacks dignity and creates a climate of fear throughout an organization. Its tone is not appropriate for a professional atmosphere.

☐ *"I don't like surprises."*
This commonly used phrase seems reasonably benign and useful. However, it often leads to many decisions being pushed up too high—an impediment to innovation and initiative on the part of associates.

☐ *"My door is always open."*
In many small organizations, this statement can be true and, therefore, appropriate. However, leaders of large organizations who use it frequently are misleading their associates. If you are the leader of a large organization and your door really does remain open (that is, if you make yourself available at all times), then you probably

will become buried in minutiae. And if you say your door is always open and it is not, you will soon find that you have created an atmosphere of cynicism and skepticism about your availability to associates.

☐ *"Be sure to keep me informed."*
Here is a sure-fire way to ensure an overly full in-box and lots of phone calls, both day and night. The phrase is the antithesis of delegation and the empowerment of associates—two key principles in leading medium-sized and large organizations.

☐ *"Just give me the bottom line."*
Bosses who use this phrase are often beginning to lose touch with the essential elements of important issues. A better phrase is, "I need the bottom line, but I also need to understand how you got there."

☐ *"We can't handle any new initiatives this year."*
This kind of guidance is counterproductive to taking an organization to higher levels of good planning, competence, and efficiency. If you refuse new approaches and ideas because of budgetary or other reasons, you may be making a major mistake. If you actively engage in divestiture work which unloads activities that are no longer needed, you ought to be able to develop, encourage, and implement new initiatives every year.

☐ *"If it ain't broke, don't fix it."*
This commonly used phrase seems to make a great deal of sense. However, it is often an impediment to progress and an invitation to mediocrity. Innovation and initiative are helpful not only to faltering organizations, but also to ones that are running well. If it's not broken, it's still worth improving.

☐ *"My mind is closed on that issue."*
This is an unwise phrase on two counts. First, your mind should *never* be totally closed on *any* issue, since changing circumstances or new data may require a readdressal of issues. Second, the phrase sends a signal of great rigidity.

❏ *"I'll call in every morning to get an update."*
If you cannot go on a trip or holiday without checking with the office on a daily basis, you are making a very important statement about your approach to leadership; you are saying that you do not have confidence in the team and the system that you have set up. If something really important occurs and you have trained your people well, they will call you. Why not let your deputy or assistant run the show for a few days? It may do you, your company, and your deputy a lot of good. This is called leadership development. It also is called trust.

❏ *"Let's agonize over this issue."*
This phrase is disliked by associates for obvious reasons. Better phrases are, "Let's brainstorm this issue," and "Let's build a decision matrix on this issue." Decision-making should be a challenging experience; normally, it should not be an agonizing or painful one.

❏ *"There is no way a woman [black, Latino, unmarried person, etc.] will get that job."*
Discrimination on the part of the leader has a very serious impact. Sexual, racial, cultural, ethnic, or any other prejudice on the part of the leader transmits immediately throughout the organization. Even a small amount of subtle discrimination at the top can lead to major injustices and many morale problems at lower levels.

❏ *"This organization was in bad shape until eighteen [twelve, twenty-four, ...] months ago."*
If it was eighteen months ago that you took charge, you have just revealed a great deal about yourself, your ego, and your objectivity. Your message is that the previous boss must have been a lousy leader; that the staff and subordinate leaders are not capable of excellent performance unless they are blessed with you as their boss; and that if you should leave for another job, retire, or die, the place will probably fall apart. A more magnanimous (and probably more accurate) way to discuss the subject would be to say, "The last boss was super and the plans she put

together were first-rate. I am pleased that I have the kind of team that can carry out these plans and take the organization to even higher levels of excellence."

---

14. Planning Checklist

One of your major responsibilities as a leader is to establish a strategic vision for the organization. A plans office and an institutionalized planning system can be of wonderful assistance in this regard. In addition, the following questions can help you to organize a thorough strategic plan.

- ❐ What are my organization's major plans?

- ❐ When was the last time I reviewed them?

- ❐ How large is the planning staff?

- ❐ Does the planning staff report directly to the top leader? If not, why not?

- ❐ Is there a pre-existing strategic plan?
     —how is it used and by whom?
     —if not, what is the strategic vision of the organization?

- ❐ Does my planning system include:
     —personnel planning?
     —resource planning?
     —facility/construction planning?
     —logistics planning?
     —operational planning?
     —contingency planning?
     —opportunity planning?
     —economic planning?
     —investment planning?

- ❐ What is the staff relationship between the chief planner and:
     —the chief of human resources?
     —the chief of logistics?
     —the chief of finance?
     —the chief of operations?
     —the chief of information technology?
     —the field organizations?

❏ What kind of divestiture and reevaluation of priorities is taking place?

❏ What major innovations are underway?

❏ How often is there a planning/innovation off-site seminar?

❏ Are there regular scheduled meetings between myself and the strategic planners?
  —do these meetings lead to any decisions?

❏ Who is responsible for carrying out any decisions that might impact the long-range future of the organization?

❏ At what points in the future should I revisit each major decision?

15. Thank You Checklist

These are a few ways to thank the people who do so much to make your organization thrive.

Many thanks for:

❏ your contribution to the mission.

❏ your integrity.

❏ your commitment to excellence.

❏ setting and maintaining high standards.

❏ your leadership.

❏ your teachership.

❏ meeting our goals.

❏ exceeding our goals.

❏ your marvelous attitude.

❏ your willingness to take on the tough jobs.

❏ your willingness to work cooperatively with people.

❏ your honesty.

❏ your willingness to "tell it like it is."

❏ your willingness to take risks.

❏ your courage.

❏ your self-sacrifice.

❏ your creativity.

❏ your ideas.

❏ your vision.

❏ your cerebral energy.

❏ your ability to conceptualize.

- ❏ your receptivity to ideas.
- ❏ your sound advice.
- ❏ your common sense.
- ❏ your style.
- ❏ adding elegance and style to our organization.
- ❏ your maturity.
- ❏ your lack of pettiness.
- ❏ your tolerance.
- ❏ your courtesy.
- ❏ your sincerity.
- ❏ your trust.
- ❏ your sensitivity.
- ❏ your loyalty.
- ❏ your love.
- ❏ your dedication.
- ❏ your responsiveness.
- ❏ your professionalism.
- ❏ your ability to rise above parochialism.
- ❏ your willingness to criticize constructively.
- ❏ your ability to think and act strategically.
- ❏ your willingness to help others.
- ❏ your magnanimity.
- ❏ caring.
- ❏ making my job easy.

16. Crisis Leadership Checklist

The best leaders anticipate crises and prevent many of them from occurring. However, some crises cannot be anticipated and others cannot be prevented. Leading an organization successfully through a crisis is often very challenging. But it can also be an uplifting and strengthening experience for you and for your people. The following guidelines may help.

- ❒ Have a transition plan that shifts you from normal operations to crisis situation gear.
- ❒ Quickly set up a work shift pattern. For example, establish twelve-hour shifts. (CNN and many military units move immediately into twelve-hour shifts.)
- ❒ Make decisions quickly, but responsibly.
- ❒ Keep everything simple; don't give complex directions.
- ❒ Be flexible.
- ❒ Do not demand exactness or perfection.
- ❒ Expect things to get fouled up, and don't overreact when they do.
- ❒ Focus your attention on the next few days; don't "manage" the crisis minute by minute.
- ❒ Form an "opportunity" team and:
    —meet with this team at least once a day to get its ideas.
    —consider actions that could not be taken in a normal situation.
- ❒ Get adequate rest; over time, eighteen-hour days will diminish your performance and your objectivity.
- ❒ Get near the action.
- ❒ Set some priorities and:
    —articulate them to your associates.
    —follow them.

☐ Develop a public affairs strategy.

☐ Keep in close contact with your lawyer and your public affairs expert.

☐ If there are adversaries:
 —outsmart them.
 —operate within their decision cycles.

☐ Thank people often.

☐ Keep training, if you can.

☐ Maintain high standards of ethics and dignity; sniff the air on a regular basis.

---

17. Press Conference and Media Interview Checklist

With the explosive growth of the media in recent years, it is not just heads of state, foreign dignitaries, senators, governors, mayors, generals, and CEOs of major corporations that meet regularly with reporters and journalists. Leaders at many levels must be prepared to interact, often on short notice, with the media. This checklist can be a useful guide as you prepare for your next interview or press conference.

❐ Am I the correct person to face the press?
  —if not, can I pick someone else without being accused of "ducking the press"?

❐ Do I have a written statement to give or to read to the media?
  —have I studied it closely to be sure that it conforms to policy and that I am comfortable with it?

❐ Who will be there?
  —what are their backgrounds, biases, and reputations for fairness?
  —are any of them the cynical police-reporter type?

❐ If an interview, will it be on or off the record?

❐ If a press conference, how long will it last?
  —how will it be terminated?

❐ Will television cameras be there?
  —will it be live or on tape?

❐ Will I get to see a copy of the manuscript or an edited television tape?

❐ What agenda do I wish to pursue?

❐ What is my reputation with the press?

❐ What is my organization's reputation with the press?

❐ What have I done recently, and what has my organization

done recently, that is particularly noteworthy?

❏ What tough questions can I expect and on what issues?
—what are good answers to these questions?

❏ What issues are particularly sensitive ones for my boss?

❏ What mistakes have been made by spokespersons in my organization that I wish to correct?

❏ Are there any skeletons in my closet?
—if so, am I prepared to be confronted with tough questions about my personal or professional conduct?

❏ If I expect a hostile session, what approach have I devised to reduce the hostility?
—has my staff offered any suggestions?
—have I considered the use of humor?

---

18. Risk-Taking Checklist

While management is, to a considerable extent, the avoidance of risk, leadership requires risk-taking. Good planning and the creation of an implementation strategy always should precede a risk. Keep in mind the bottom line of risk-taking: if you don't fail on occasion, you are not pushing the boundaries of innovation hard enough.

How to Take Prudent Risks

- ❏ Get some good ideas:
  —brainstorm with your associates; subcontractors; consultants; and customers.
  —develop a plan.
  —put together implementation strategies.
  —anticipate expected and unexpected consequences:
    —ask the "what if" questions.

- ❏ In a close call on whether to risk or not, do it.

What to Do When the Risk Succeeds

- ❏ Throw a party.

- ❏ Congratulate your people.

- ❏ Pass out several awards.

- ❏ Let your peers know what you learned.

- ❏ Try something more risky soon.

What to Do When the Risk Fails

- ❏ Tell the boss immediately.

- ❏ Accept the blame.

- ❏ Analyze reasons for the failure.

- ❏ Celebrate the failure.

- ❏ Take another risk soon.

Various Approaches to Risk-Taking

- ☐ Do something—don't tell any of the bosses.
- ☐ Send the boss a note: "I am about to do X . . ., if I don't hear from you by this Friday, I am pressing on."
- ☐ Violate the rules, but let the boss know when and why.
- ☐ Send a letter to the top boss—then press on.

19. Divestiture Checklist

All organizations eventually will become obsolete unless divestiture planning takes place on a regular basis. Opportunities should be sought actively to close down obsolete plants, to disestablish offices that no longer contribute significantly to the mission, to discontinue product lines that are losing market appeal, and to unload technologically antiquated systems. To carry out effective, responsible divestiture, ask the below-listed questions.

❐ What are the principal advantages of this divestiture?

❐ What are the principal disadvantages of this divestiture?

❐ What short-term and long-term impact will this divestiture have on the mission of the organization?
　　—will the short-term disadvantages be outweighed by the long-term advantages?

❐ How much money, personnel, and other resources will be saved as a result of this divestiture?
　　—how easy will it be to transfer these resources into more productive areas?

❐ What impact will this divestiture have on the overall philosophy, priorities, and goals of this organization?
　　—will the goals, priorities, and philosophy of the organization have to be changed as a result of this divestiture?

❐ Do I have the authority to make this decision myself?

❐ With whom should I consult before I make my decision?

❐ Should I meet with an outside consultant to get a disinterested opinion on the wisdom of this divestiture proposal?

❐ What are the alternative means by which this divestiture can be implemented?
　　—which scheme is the best scheme?

❐ How will this divestiture be perceived by the employees throughout the organization?

    —will it be interpreted as being the first of a number of divestiture steps that may threaten many jobs throughout the organization?

❐ Which individuals will lose their jobs?

    —how involved should I be in counselling them and finding them attractive new job opportunities?

❐ Does this divestiture provide opportunities to do other important things, such as reorganization, removing incompetent employees, etc.?

❐ What are the various ways in which resources that are saved can be applied to other areas within the organization?

    —what way is the best way?

❐ How should the decision be announced?

    —should I do it myself?

    —if not, who should do it?

20. Change Leadership Checklist

Leading an organization or an institution through times of change is challenging and often stressful. However, the process can be exciting if you are well-prepared and have confidence in your strategy. The following statements should serve as helpful pointers when you are dealing with a period of change. I am indebted to Shiela Sheinberg for many of the points in this list.

❐ Hierarchy is out; long live adhocracy.

❐ Functions are out; processes are in. Down with the walls!

❐ Relationships are crucial: interfacing; partnering.

❐ No more heroes; teamwork is key.

❐ Employees are volunteers, not hostages.

❐ Expect exceptional performance from everyone; we get what we expect.

❐ The organization is no longer the center; the customer is the center of the universe.

❐ Challenge "business as usual":
   —change and continuous improvement are vital to a successful future.
   —risk-taking is essential.
   —if it ain't broke, break it.

❐ Leadership comes first, not management; visioning is more important than your in-box.

❐ Quality or else; do the right thing at the right time.

❐ Communication is the core; everyone has a right to be heard.

❐ A changing organization is a learning organization; don't become a prisoner of an antiquated paradigm.

❐ Lovers of change win.

21. Promotion Board Checklist

This checklist was created by Admiral J. S. Gracey when he was the Commandant of the Coast Guard.

To promotion board members: in selecting future leaders, ask your-selves the following questions about each person.

Is this person:

- ❏ a self starter?
- ❏ a professional?
- ❏ willing to go out on a limb?
- ❏ willing to walk the extra mile?
- ❏ courteous and considerate, especially to/of juniors?
- ❏ biased in any way?
- ❏ afraid of making a mistake?
- ❏ socially active and adept? (Is his or her spouse socially active and adept, as well?)
- ❏ strong only in his or her own "specialty," or can he or she contribute in the whole range of activities in the firm [service, agency]?
- ❏ willing to try new things, even at some risk?
- ❏ practical and realistic?
- ❏ warm and personable?
- ❏ capable of being a maverick? (Does he or she always insist on being a maverick?)
- ❏ perceptive?
- ❏ innovative?

Does this person:

- ❏ tell me what he or she thinks I want to hear?

☐ not tell me what he or she thinks I don't want to hear?

☐ make service to the institution the number one priority, despite personal sacrifice?

☐ have a love affair going with his or her organization?

☐ set a good example in all respects?

☐ think of the wants and needs of individuals and of their families?

☐ suffer from "Chicken Littleism"?

☐ meet the public well?

☐ get awed by "big wheels," or is he or she at ease with them?

☐ let concern for his or her "future" govern his or her actions?

☐ understand the government, how it works, and how to work in it?

☐ understand Congress and how to work with congresspeople?

☐ express himself or herself well on paper and orally?

☐ understand the organization that he or she serves?

☐ understand his or her institution's role in government and its relations with state and local governments?

☐ understand his or her institution's role in community and business affairs?

☐ make things happen?

☐ get things done?

☐ lead, not push?

☐ make a good team with his or her spouse, in representing the institution he or she serves?

☐ have imagination?

☐ worry about who gets the credit?

❏ praise his or her people?

❏ go to bat for his or her people?

Will this person:

❏ disagree with me when he or she thinks I am wrong?

❏ stand up and be counted?

Can this person:

❏ "walk with kings, and not lose the common touch"?

❏ handle a huge workload and not lose the bubble?

❏ keep twelve oranges in the air at once and not drop any?

❏ accept the ideas of others?

❏ convey his or her ideas to others . . . and sell them?

❏ laugh at himself or herself?

❏ laugh at all—i.e., does he or she have a good sense of humor?

❏ deal with the press and other media?

❏ walk in another person's shoes, no matter how big or small?

❏ make a speech to which people will listen?

❏ sort out problems and keep priorities straight?

❏ hit a golfball in a shower stall and not get beaned?

❏ think on his or her feet?

❏ be tough when necessary?

❏ take an unpopular, but necessary, stand and stick to it?

❏ grasp new concepts quickly?

❏ identify problems (vs. symptoms) . . . and get them solved?

❏ find a new course if the one he or she has selected comes a cropper?

❏ get "lost" in the infamous, single-tree "impenetrable forest"?

❏ make decisions? *Does* he or she make them?

❏ handle pressure?

❏ inspire others?

Would I want to work with this person as a fellow leader?

Has this person got "class"?

---

22. Congressional Visit Checklist

This checklist provides helpful questions for you to consider if/when a congressperson or a staff member from Congress is coming to visit your organization. The below-listed items do not necessarily require action, but will serve as reminders of those areas that need to be reviewed. This checklist is a modification of one that was prepared by Wilson R. Rutherford, III, and Leslie F. Kenne.

❒ Am I aware of the rights of congressional members; of the sense, the direction of the Congress in session? Remember:
   —Congress is not the enemy.
   —members of Congress have a right to ask questions, and deserve my timely response.
   —it is important to know the current issues and emphases of Congress.

❒ Am I aware of the significance of the constituents and constituent interest?
   —minimize briefings to congresspeople.
   —provide a list of people who the member of Congress met personally.
   —emphasize the participation of women and minorities in my mission.

❒ Am I aware that it may be necessary to treat the staff members of Congress and members of Congress differently?
   —personal staffers manage the congressperson's office.
   —professional staffers work directly on legislation.
   —staffers can be very influential with their member of Congress.
   —staffers are issue-oriented; they want detail.
     —be truthful and objective.
     —remember that briefings to staffers can be more lengthy than those to the congresspeople.
     —provide point papers and copies of charts.
     —have experts at my briefings to provide concise information and to answer questions.

—keep the number of your people at the briefings small.
—members of Congress tend to be generalists, more
interested in orientation than in details.
  —make briefings few and short.
  —provide an overview of the mission.
  —speak in layperson's terms; avoid acronyms.
  —give windshield and walking tours.
  —provide hands-on demonstrations.
—members of Congress are usually interested in meeting constituents.

❐ Am I well aware of the issues to be discussed? Do I know
what factors to consider in my discussion?
  —primary versus secondary issues.
  —my agenda versus that of my organization; the organization's agenda normally has higher priority.
  —the Washington, DC, agenda.
  —institutional priorities on issues.
  —the various sides of the issues.
  —the need to show things in a balanced way.

❐ Am I aware that my attitude is all-important to a successful visit?
  —be careful to avoid personality conflicts.
  —be responsive.
  —remain nonpartisan.
  —don't try to "snow" anybody.
  —be candid and honest (*never* mislead).
  —caveat personal opinions.
  —don't shoot from the hip.
  —know the politics of the district/state.
  —put myself in the congressperson's shoes.
  —be careful in advancing my own agenda.
  —be enthusiastic and positive.

❐ Have I coordinated the visit with the appropriate agencies?
  —received guidance from the agency or corporate office
  for legislative affairs?
  —obtained background information from corporate
  headquarters or legislative affairs in Washington, DC?

—gotten local community leaders and government officials involved; cultivated their support?

—ensured functional area coordination between my office and corporate headquarters?

—let my boss know how the visit went; related any unplanned incident and any major mistakes that I have made?

23. Congressional Testimony Checklist

Because of the large increase in the number of Congressional committees and subcommittees, the tendency of members of Congress to hold more and more hearings, and the proliferation of political issues (particularly in the financial, environmental, and social welfare areas), the chances of leaders being called upon to testify before Congress have increased dramatically. I developed the following checklist after having testified as a principal witness before many committees and subcommittees of both Houses of the United States Congress.

❑ Before which committee or subcommittee am I testifying?

❑ In which hearing room?

❑ Will the hearing be open or closed?

❑ Will the hearing be televised?

❑ Which members of Congress and key staffers are expected to attend?
  —what points of view, constituent interests, and biases can I expect from *each* congressperson, and from *each* key staffer?

❑ Which members of Congress are likely to be hostile?
  —why and on what issues?

❑ Are "prepared remarks" appropriate?
  —have they been fully coordinated?
  —have they been submitted at least forty-eight hours ahead of time?
  —am I ready to summarize the prepared remarks in a very few minutes?

❑ Is there an opportunity to submit questions ahead of time that the chairperson or someone else might ask of me?
  —if so, have the questions been submitted?
  —have I thought through the answers to these questions?

❐ Are there any other principal witnesses?
    —have I met with them ahead of time?
    —if not, can I arrange to meet with them a few minutes
    before testimony to coordinate?

24. Rules of Thumb for Congressional Testimony

So many of the people who testify before the U.S. Congress fail to understand some basic factors. My rules of thumb may be helpful as you prepare for your first (or next) opportunity to testify on Capitol Hill.

- ❏ Never lie, for two reasons: it is wrong and it is dumb. You will surely get caught if you lie and, once caught, you will ruin your reputation with the Congress for the rest of your professional life.

- ❏ Do not read your opening statement.
    —submit it for the record and summarize it in three to five minutes.

- ❏ Be prepared.
    —reading and skull sessions with your staff are very helpful.

- ❏ Give brief answers to the questions.

- ❏ Be respectful to members of Congress.
    —although particular individuals may not be too sharp, the institution deserves your respect.
    —an arrogant witness is never a successful witness.

- ❏ Be aware of specific constituency interests on the part of congresspeople.

- ❏ Never arrive late to a hearing.
    —better an hour early than five minutes late.

- ❏ As members of Congress and staffers wander into the hearing room prior to the hearing, approach them, introduce yourself to them, and remind them where you have met in the past.

- ❏ Do not allow yourself to be intimidated.
    —if a member of Congress badgers you, listen quietly until the statement is over, and then quietly, but force-

fully, state your position; point out, in specific terms, where the congressperson may be in error.

❒ Do not interrupt a member of Congress.

❒ If you do not know the answer to the question, say: "I will submit an answer for the record."

❒ If you generally know the answer but are not sure of every detail, do your best to answer it. (If you say "I'll submit an answer for the record" too many times, you will not be a very credible or effective witness.)

❒ If you promise to do something while you are testifying (to conduct a study, to provide data, etc.), do it promptly.

❒ Be sensitive about time and scheduling with the committee.

❒ Do not bring a large number of back-up witnesses.
   —you will appear to be much more in charge if you testify alone.

25. Telltale Phrases to Listen For

As a leader, you need to have your antennae out, to gather information from all directions, and to detect dangers before they hit. It is important for you to be aware of patterns within your organization, to be open to feedback and to criticism, and to listen to your subordinate leaders. Listen for the following key phrases; they may indicate trouble.

Unethical phrases:

- ❏ "fudging the figures"
- ❏ "cooking the numbers"
- ❏ "gaming the program"
- ❏ "bending the rules"
- ❏ "manipulating the data"
- ❏ "pencil whipping"

Careerist phrases:

- ❏ "I don't trust the personnel system."
- ❏ "Who is your sponsor?"
- ❏ "I don't have a sponsor."
- ❏ "You need to get on board."
- ❏ "I need to get my ticket punched."
- ❏ "It's not what you know, it's who you know."
- ❏ "I need some face time with the boss."
- ❏ "I want a high visibility job."
- ❏ "Joe 'talks a good game.'"
- ❏ "To get ahead, you have got to go along."
- ❏ "You need to quit 'fighting the problem.'"
- ❏ "Be careful—the boss likes to 'shoot the messenger.'"

Phrases indicating that either the Peter or the Paul Principle (see pages 126-127) is at work:

- ❏ "It sure takes X a long time to get something done."
- ❏ "Why can't Y seem to focus on the issue?"
- ❏ "Z will never take a position on anything."
- ❏ "Have you noticed that X is always defensive?"
- ❏ "Y has no initiative."
- ❏ "Z has lost his [her] drive."
- ❏ "X was a great staff member, but seems lost as a leader."
- ❏ "Y's folks are afraid of her [him]."
- ❏ "Z's people are frustrated."
- ❏ "X has had a bad case of 'not invented here' and is never open to ideas from the outside."
- ❏ "Y seems to complain all the time."
- ❏ "Z is on the road a lot—I wonder who is minding the store?"
- ❏ "X never seems to make any deadlines."
- ❏ "Is that job too big for Y?"
- ❏ "Z is out of touch."
- ❏ "How come X surrounds himself [herself] with cronies?"
- ❏ "Y lets the system screw over her [his] people."
- ❏ "Z has no sense of outrage."

26. Cynical Expressions to Listen For

By carefully listening as you travel the halls and offices of the organization, you can pick up cynical expressions that may tell a lot about the organizational climate and your leadership style. This list identifies common cynical expressions and explains the perceptions that most likely lurk behind each of them.

☐ *"When is the ten o'clock meeting going to begin?"*
The implied message is that you are a poor time manager and have a bad reputation for falling behind schedule. Your associates may feel that you are wasting their time, as they cool their heels in the outer office. They also may think that you have no grasp of the fact that they, too, have schedules to follow; many of them will have coworkers and customers waiting to meet with them.

☐ *"I wonder how those folks in the other departments avoid Saturday work call?"*
You may be a workaholic who is guilty of calling in a lot of people for weekend work that is not necessary. Associates need their weekends to unwind and recharge.

☐ *"When is the boss going on his next trip?"*
There could be a number of different signals here. Your associates may be suggesting that they want you out of town so that they can get something worthwhile done, or so that they can get a day or two with their families. Another possibility is that they are wondering why you are doing so much traveling and so little productive work.

☐ *"It is impossible to fire anyone around here."*
You appear guilty of protecting employees to the point that you are tolerating a number of incompetents in your organization. The phrase may signify that you have not supported your subordinate leaders when they have tried to fire somebody who was incompetent or unethical.

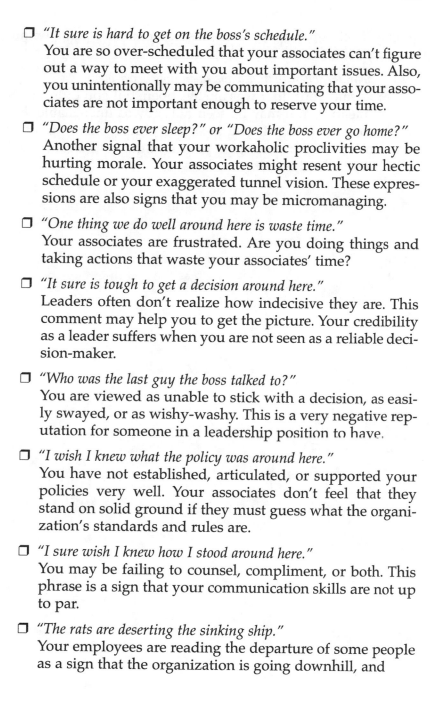

❏ *"It sure is hard to get on the boss's schedule."*
You are so over-scheduled that your associates can't figure out a way to meet with you about important issues. Also, you unintentionally may be communicating that your associates are not important enough to reserve your time.

❏ *"Does the boss ever sleep?" or "Does the boss ever go home?"*
Another signal that your workaholic proclivities may be hurting morale. Your associates might resent your hectic schedule or your exaggerated tunnel vision. These expressions are also signs that you may be micromanaging.

❏ *"One thing we do well around here is waste time."*
Your associates are frustrated. Are you doing things and taking actions that waste your associates' time?

❏ *"It sure is tough to get a decision around here."*
Leaders often don't realize how indecisive they are. This comment may help you to get the picture. Your credibility as a leader suffers when you are not seen as a reliable decision-maker.

❏ *"Who was the last guy the boss talked to?"*
You are viewed as unable to stick with a decision, as easily swayed, or as wishy-washy. This is a very negative reputation for someone in a leadership position to have.

❏ *"I wish I knew what the policy was around here."*
You have not established, articulated, or supported your policies very well. Your associates don't feel that they stand on solid ground if they must guess what the organization's standards and rules are.

❏ *"I sure wish I knew how I stood around here."*
You may be failing to counsel, compliment, or both. This phrase is a sign that your communication skills are not up to par.

❏ *"The rats are deserting the sinking ship."*
Your employees are reading the departure of some people as a sign that the organization is going downhill, and

quickly. Such a perception can cause concern and panic within the organization.

❑ *"I wonder when that 'always-open door' ever opens."*
    You said your door was always open, but you didn't real-
    ly mean it. You may be seen not only as unavailable, but
    also as insincere. If you hear this phrase, there's a lot of
    work to be done to regain your reputation as a concerned
    and involved leader.

27. Useful Short Phrases for Leaders

Short, powerful phrases are an effective way to make a point, pay a compliment, ask for feedback, take the blame for failure, ease the level of tension, etc. The following is a list of phrases that you may find helpful in dealing with associates, in making decisions, and in disciplining yourself.

- ❐ "I don't know."
- ❐ "How am I wasting your time?"
- ❐ "Give it to me straight, folks—what did I do wrong?"
- ❐ "I made a mistake."
- ❐ "I was wrong."
- ❐ "Let's get back to basics."
- ❐ "First things first."
- ❐ "Perhaps it is time for me to take another look at my position on that issue."
- ❐ "This setback was my fault. I didn't give you the support you needed."
- ❐ "Let's go on a jog together and we can discuss it—you can talk and I will breathe."
- ❐ "I know some of you are uncomfortable with this decision. I will take full responsibility if we fail."
- ❐ "Let's try it."
- ❐ "Let's go for it."
- ❐ "Well done!"
- ❐ "Well, it didn't work, but I'm sure glad we gave it a try!"
- ❐ "Your wise counsel has been very useful. Please forgive me for not following it this time."
- ❐ "It's six o'clock, let's all go home."

❏ "What good books have you read lately?"

❏ "Let's include the spouses [families] in this."

❏ "I'll be gone a month; don't worry about giving me up-dates."

❏ "Help me discipline my in-box; don't send me issues that you can decide."

❏ "I have become part of the problem. I am stepping down so that someone less committed to the past can take over this dynamic organization."

❏ "Our great success was your success. Please don't give me the credit."

❏ "You are responsible for my success."

❏ "I'm proud of you."

❏ "You're the best."

❏ "We need you."

❏ "We treasure you."

---

28. Useful Phrases for Confident Associates

Associates need to be frank and candid with their bosses or else the organization will suffer. But it is important to be quite diplomatic at times. Finding the right phrase and finding the right time to use it can be quite a challenge. Here are a few useful statements.

- ❒ "Please tell me what to do, not how to do it."
- ❒ "Let's go for it!"
- ❒ "Life's full of risks, so let's take one!"
- ❒ "We can't afford *not* to do this."
- ❒ "This initiative could be your legacy."
- ❒ "This will give us a big edge over our competition."
- ❒ "The time to decide is now."
- ❒ "Before we go with this, I suggest we run it by our lawyer."
- ❒ "If we decide to do this, our folks will love [hate] you."
- ❒ "If you decide to go this route, you might just as well fire Sam [Sue]. You will have destroyed his [her] credibility with his [her] employees."
- ❒ "History will judge us kindly [severely] if we do this."
- ❒ "The Board of Directors will go bananas when they learn about this."
- ❒ "The press sure will have fun with this one."
- ❒ "I wonder which one of our departments will leak this story first?"
- ❒ "It just won't work."
- ❒ "There ain't no way."
- ❒ "It sure doesn't jibe with our strategic plan."
- ❒ "It won't go down well on the production line."

❑ "If I do that for you, I won't be able to sleep at night."

❑ "Of course, our competitors are doing it, but we have higher standards."

❑ "If you 'want it bad,' you will 'get it bad'; let's give the staff another week."

---

29. Thoughts for All Seasons

There are some truisms that can't be defined as guidelines, but still are useful for you, as a leader or as a subordinate associate. I suggest that you read them from time to time, using them to trigger both motivation and discipline in yourself.

- ❑ *"The perfect is the enemy of the good."*
  When a leader seeks perfection, he or she often gets just the opposite. Very good solutions are often better than perfect solutions, particularly when the perfect solutions can't be found until three months too late. A very good strategy tends to be cheaper, faster, and easier to implement than a perfect strategy.

- ❑ *"Sir, it's time to blow up the bridge."*
  Bridge on the River Kwai, the Academy Award-winning movie of 1957, demonstrates with great clarity the dangers of rigid planning. It was correct for the British and American prisoners of war to build the bridge for their Japanese captors; it was also correct to blow it up when the Japanese train arrived. How often have we watched good policy evolve into bad policy, and yet find changing it to be awfully hard?

- ❑ *"It won't go down on the production line."*
  An idea, procedure, or approach may seem great in the corporate boardroom. However, if it won't work on the production line, in the field, or in the sales office, it's time to take another look. Be sure to cover all bases before a plan is implemented.

- ❑ *"If you want it bad, you'll get it bad."*
  A clever put-down by an associate who is trying to convince the boss or a coworker that a short deadline will lead to poor results. Often, the "haste makes waste" adage rings true.

- ❑ *"A good manager does things right. A leader does the right things."*

This quote from Warren Bennis captures a fundamental difference between management and leadership. Great leaders are superb at both management *and* leadership; but, when in doubt, they always emphasize leadership over management.

❐ *"Management is about systems, controls, procedures, policies, structure. Leadership is about trust, about allowing yourself to be vulnerable, and about caring for people."*
Once again, I have borrowed Warren Bennis' thoughts to emphasize some of the essential elements of leadership. The true leader does more than be in charge; he or she learns from, encourages, and rewards motivation, creativity, innovation, achievement, and good morale.

30. Blazing Flashes of the Obvious

When I am asked to give a short speech on leadership, I often share with the audience my "Blazing Flashes of the Obvious." I have collected these "BFOs" from many sources over many years. I hope these "one liners" will serve as helpful reminders—*rules and tools*—as you carry out your role as a leader and a helper of people.

- ❏ Keep your ego under tight control, and don't forget to check it at the door.
- ❏ Develop mental toughness.
- ❏ Be brutally honest with yourself and with your bosses.
- ❏ Be magnanimous.
- ❏ Share your time, your talent, and your compassion.
- ❏ Squint with your ears.
- ❏ Learn from and be strengthened by failure.
- ❏ Identify, nurture, and protect the innovators.
- ❏ Be decisive.
- ❏ Don't become indispensable.
- ❏ Don't let others become indispensable.
- ❏ Avoid the cowardice of silence; when it is time to speak up, do so.
- ❏ Thank people creatively and often.
- ❏ Observe, thank, and reward the invisible people.
- ❏ Help bosses become better leaders.
- ❏ Be proactive.
- ❏ Don't waste people's time.
- ❏ Develop a mindset of servant leadership.

❏ Question people imaginatively.

❏ Be ambitious to do, not to be.

❏ Criticize up, praise down.

❏ Reduce your health age through mental and physical fitness.

❏ Develop solid leadership skills and techniques concerning:
  —listening. (This is the most important skill.)
  —speed reading.
  —answering mail.
  —disciplining the in-box/schedule/telephone.
  —running a meeting.
  —dictation. (Consider voice recognition software.)

❏ Avoid the lurk of cronyism, and don't allow yourself to be someone's crony.

❏ Help your people understand you; share your "pet peeve" list with your associates.

❏ Seek simplicity—but then mistrust it.

❏ Every year, take your folks on an off-site retreat.

❏ Smoke out those of low integrity.

❏ If something unethical is happening, correct it *now*.

❏ Manage the intangibles.

❏ Enjoy your work; don't have a furrowed brow.

❏ Inspire people to do their very best.

❏ Concentrate on performance and process, not just on results.

❏ Maintain a sense of outrage.

❏ Beware of those who would intimidate you.

❏ Get rid of the fat.

❏ Be willing to practice mortuary leadership—that is, divest pieces of your organization that have become obsolescent or irrelevant.

☐ Avoid the activity trap; remember that hyperactivity usually leads to strategic drift.

☐ Set specific goals and specific priorities; avoid using generalized goals in no priority order.

☐ Go for the small wins.

☐ Rise above office politics.

☐ Be a "worry buster."

☐ Start meetings on time.

☐ End meetings on time or early.

☐ Answer your mail promptly, following the "Colin Powell rule" (page 116); answer all letters within 72 hours, and angry letters within 24 hours.

☐ Encourage creative tension.

☐ Avoid facile consensus and "group think."

☐ Learn how to "look around corners."

☐ Anticipate crises and head them off at the pass.

☐ If crisis does come, be a creative crisis manager.

☐ Be a courageous leader; have the courage to begin, to continue, to prevail.

☐ Pick a role model to emulate—for example, George Marshall; Eleanor Roosevelt; Harry Truman; Larraine Matusak; Madeleine Albright; Colin Powell; Jimmie Dyess; Mother Teresa.

☐ Pick a negative role model, from whom you learn what *not* to do—for example, Robert McNamara; Warren Harding; George McClellan.

☐ Pick an organizational role model or two.

☐ Attend a leadership development program. (See Appendix D.)

❏ Do some serious reading on leadership and management; read at least six leadership books per year.

❏ Never travel without two books to read.

❏ On those long commutes, listen to audiotapes on leadership, strategic thinking, or ethics.

❏ Trust your instincts and your impulses.

❏ If something smells bad, take some more sniffs; do not overlook situations that seem suspicious.

❏ Don't become a prisoner of your own paradigm.

❏ Fight the tendency to clone yourself.

❏ Hire your people very carefully.

❏ Surround yourself with people who are smarter and more creative than you.

❏ Establish a 360° feedback system; ensure that all leaders get feedback from their bosses, peers, and subordinate associates.

❏ Don't be just a leader of people and resources.

❏ Don't be just a manager of people and resources; be a leader of ideas. Watch for and share the "Oh, wow!"s.

❏ Favor action over analysis.

❏ Favor trust over rules; when necessary, throw out the rule book.

❏ Avoid sending out "I don't trust you" messages.

❏ Learn from other subcultures.

❏ Learn from the military, the non-profit organizations, and from corporations.

❏ Seek out the entrepreneurs and the intrapreneurs.

❏ Practice forgiveness; forgive others and forgive yourself.

❏ Beware of certainty.

❏ Have a "decent doubt."

❏ Don't spend too much time with the malcontents. It only encourages them.

❏ When it is time to let someone go, get on with it.

❏ Don't always demand perfection.

❏ Be willing to make exceptions to policy.

❏ Create a need (or a market) and fill it. For examples, study Ted Turner, Fred Smith, Bill Gates, and Steve Jobs.

❏ Push your organization up the wisdom pyramid; take it from data to information, to knowledge, to wisdom.

❏ Don't become transfixed with detail.

❏ Fight against paranoia.

❏ Welcome criticism; remember that loyalty and criticism are mutually supporting.

❏ Avoid the defensive crouch.

❏ Never attribute to malice that which is explained adequately by stupidity.

❏ Acknowledge and announce your mistakes quickly.

❏ Remember, bad news does not improve with time.

❏ Use the CNN model of acknowledging and fixing errors. (See page 166.)

❏ Tolerate those who have "love quarrels" with you and/or your organization.

❏ Don't set unreasonable deadlines.

❏ Remember the iron law of unexpected consequences.

❏ Think through the downsides of your decisions.

❏ Establish and nurture a braintrust of 200 to 300 smart folks.

❏ Establish self-reinforcing relationships.

❐ Follow the French code: liberty, equality, and *fraternity*.

❐ Look for solutions that reconcile the opposites.

❐ Follow the platinum rule: treat others the way they would like to be treated.

❐ Be a leader developer; practice "mentorship plus."

❐ Help your people think like your boss.

❐ Be someone's hero.

❐ Encourage risk-taking.

❐ Don't accept good enough as good enough.

❐ Don't postpone joy; if there is something to celebrate, do it *now*.

❐ Be of good cheer.

❐ Use your wit to amuse, not abuse.

❐ Deal creatively with the dark side of people.

❐ Watch out for the sociopaths.

❐ Downsize with care and understanding.

❐ Invent the future.

❐ Join the World Future Society. Both its annual conventions and its magazine, *The Futurist*, will help your strategic thinking. (Call 1–301–656–8274)

❐ Regularly read the following magazines: *The Economist; Business Week; The Futurist*.

❐ Wear out, don't rust out.

❐ Don't retire on the job.

❐ Don't let others retire in place.

❐ Be a blame acceptor; don't be afraid to say:
   —"I don't know."
   —"I made a mistake."
   —"I need help."

—"I'm sorry."
—"It was my fault."

☐ Be willing to bear pain.

☐ Every day, do some networking.

☐ Stay very close to the customers, and dazzle them with surprises and delights.

☐ Help your associates find leadership metaphors.

☐ Never try to get even; avoid acts that make you look vengeful or petty.

☐ Expand your peripheral vision.

☐ Have a nose for stale air.

☐ Fight complacency constantly.

☐ Beware of success—fight smugness.

☐ Challenge jokes, language, or remarks that may offend.

☐ Give aid and support to those who are active in the community.

☐ Avoid becoming a control freak.

☐ Choose an anchor who is mature and has impeccable integrity. Hold onto that anchor during the tough times.

☐ Focus on progresses, not on form.

☐ Don't sweat the small stuff.

☐ Remember that most of it is small stuff.

☐ Expand your curiosity.

☐ Make your leadership mindset that of an orchestral conductor or a coach, not a soloist or a quarterback.

☐ Reduce the number of leader-induced problems.

☐ Seek to know why, rather than how.

☐ Give people hope.

❐ See your organization as a whole.

❐ Avoid staying inside your stovepipe for too long.

❐ Encourage others to think outside the box.

❐ Constantly look for leverage opportunities; leverage your talents, your braintrust, your time, and your technology.

❐ Trust people and make that trust predictable.

❐ Allow yourself to be vulnerable.

❐ Fight hard to stay strategic.

❐ Maintain the passion, the dream, the excitement.

APPENDIX B
case studies

We ought to be able to learn some things second hand. There is not enough time to make all the mistakes ourselves.

—Harriet Hall

The will to succeed is important, but what's more important is the will to prepare.

—Bobby Knight

Each of the following case studies is a real-life situation. Many of them happened to me, and the rest occurred to friends or colleagues. They come from a number of sources: corporations, nonprofit organizations, the federal government, local government, and the military. Although these settings are quite different, it is clear that leaders in one sector of a society can learn from the experiences of leaders in other sectors. The interaction between the leader and the associates, the ethical dilemmas, the importance of mission, and the challenges facing the leader are often quite consistent from one organization to the next. I have purposely kept the cases and their discussions brief, in order to maximize the value for busy readers. The discussions appear in Appendix C.

1. *The Alcoholic Leader*
You are the head of an organization that is responsible for the maintenance of a large number of airplanes. There are 1,600 people working for you. Over many months, one of your four subordinate leaders has demonstrated considerable problems in

working cooperatively with fellow leaders. In addition, you have observed that his speech is sometimes slurred in the afternoons. He often uses breath mints. You suspect that he may be drinking heavily during lunch; you believe he may have a drinking problem or be an alcoholic. There is no direct evidence or information, however, and his people seem to be "protecting" him. As his immediate boss, what do you do?

2. *Showdown with Your Banker*

You are the president of a large technical organization that does research for large corporations and for the government. Your organization has been in business for four years, and has grown dramatically each year. Your line of credit with your bank is $16 million. Largely because of time delays with your clients' payments, you are normally in the red from mid-October until about the first of February, and strongly in the black from then until the end of your fiscal year on the thirtieth of September.

A few days before Christmas, the president of your bank demands an urgent meeting. You and your top corporate staff meet with him. He says that there are only $3 million left of your line of credit, and that you must take draconian actions to ensure that you do not exceed the $16 million. You calmly explain to him that what is happening is normal for your kind of business, and you ask that an additional line of credit be established just in case you exceed the $16 million. The banker is adamant—he will not extend your line of credit and demands fast action. What do you do?

3. *Integrity Problems Overseas*

You are a fast-rising young executive in a very large corporation. The corporation's president has just assigned you as the president of a major subsidiary company that is located in a city on the Indian subcontinent. You will have over 600 people working for you, most of whom will be nationals of the host country. In his normally indirect, nonspecific way, the corporation's president explains that there are major problems "out there" and it is your job to fix them. Soon after you arrive, you learn that a number of the corporate officers are involved in illegal activities (that are greatly profitable for these officials). You also find that the top foreign national in this subsidiary company is indirectly involved in these illegal activities. What do you do?

4. An Associate Blows Up

You are a president of a large industrial firm. You are having a counselling session with a senior vice president. After acknowledging all the fine contributions he has made to the company over the past year, you make a couple of modest criticisms of the way he has managed two small programs. He reacts very negatively and emotionally to your criticism and feels that you are wrong on both counts. What do you do?

5. Drug Pushing by a Leader's Child

You are the president of a large overseas subsidiary of a multinational corporation. Many of your employees send their children to an international high school in the area. The local police have uncovered a marijuana ring that includes a number of students who are selling marijuana to their friends at this high school. One of the drug sellers is the son of a plant manager who works directly for you. What do you do?

6. Testifying Before Congress

You are a president of a major aerospace corporation that does a great deal of work for the Department of Defense, and you are testifying on Capitol Hill. Just before you leave your Washington office, you learn of a major testing failure of the weapons system on which you are about to testify. The committee is voting today and you know it will be very close. Your staff is offering conflicting advice. You are quite sure that none of the committee members or the Congressional staff members are aware of the test failure. During your testimony, should you discuss the issue of the test failure? If so, what do you say?

7. Dealing with Child Molestation

You are the CEO of a major newspaper chain. The sports director of one of your papers has been arrested for child molestation while under the influence of alcohol. The judge has found him guilty and has given him a heavy fine, as well as a long jail sentence. The judge suspends the jail sentence, contingent on exemplary behavior. The associate has been a brilliant reporter and sports director and never caused any problems prior to the molestation incident. What do you do?

8. Moonlighting by a Key Associate
You hired someone to start a new division in your company. In his narrow but important new field, this man has the reputation of being the finest technical person in the country. Before you hire him, he asks if he may do some teaching on the side. In an offhand manner, you grant his request. The new employee brings on a team of five others and puts together a number of proposals for potential customers. Eighteen months later, you learn that these associates have set up an independent company. They are doing a great amount of teaching on the weekends and at night. Furthermore, they are using company time to put together the course materials. The team still seems to be working hard for you, but has yet to land a contract for your company. What do you do?

9. Empowerment Problems Overseas
You have arrived at an overseas location to take over a large subsidiary of your company. The parent company has just changed its management philosophy from hierarchical to matrix management, and you will be sharing power with a number of associates. This overseas nation has a very "old world" culture, in which the top boss is king. The people at this location have little experience in matrix management. What do you do?

10. Trouble with Your Sports Fans
You are the president of a small college that has an active and successful intercollegiate sports program. You go to almost all of the major sporting events held at your campus, including all of the home football games, which usually draw a crowd of about 5,000 fans. In recent games, you have noticed thirty or forty of your students organizing obscene cheers to taunt the opposition, as well as engaging in shoving matches with each

other that, once or twice, have broken out into fist fights. What do you do?

11. Dealing with Suicide

You are the principal of a large suburban high school. The student president of the senior class, the most outstanding scholar in the entire school, has just committed suicide. What do you do?

12. Hiring the Overly Ambitious

You are the planning director of a large government agency in Washington, DC. There are a large number of civil servants throughout the country who wish to serve in this department, since promotion opportunities are very favorable and the work is interesting. As a result, it is quite common for you to get a letter or a phone call from a senior official, recommending a particular individual for employment. Over a period of about two months, you have received recommendation letters concerning the same individual from seven senior officials. Do you hire this person?

13. Keeping Secrets

You are an assistant secretary of a military department and are visiting a major city in the Midwest. The Secretary has asked you to have a session with the editorial board of the city's major newspaper. One of the journalists persistently probes you about why your service is not developing a weapons system to accomplish an important mission. You know of a program that, in fact, addresses the mission very well. However, due to highly sensitive technology, the whole program is top secret and compartmentalized. How do you handle this line of questioning?

14. Intimidation by a Union Boss

You are the mayor of a medium-sized city (with a population of about 200,000 people). A member of your fire department has accused another member of cheating on the examination that would, if passed, take him to the next rank. An investigation takes place, and it is felt that the accused individual did cheat.

The result is a recommendation that he be suspended for a year. The fire commission, which you appointed, has two basic options: to suspend the individual immediately or to wait sixty days for a court to review the case. As mayor, you have no direct jurisdiction over the commission, but you can offer advice. Early one morning, the head of the fireman's union charges into your office and demands that the suspension be withheld until the court makes its judgment. He also threatens to take all of the fire equipment in the entire city and park it in front of City Hall if he does not get his way. As mayor, what do you do?

15. *Dealing with a Death Threat*
You are the commander of a large U.S. Navy ship. You receive a call from the wife of one of the officers on your ship. She tells you that she overheard an alarming telephone conversation between her next-door neighbor and someone else; a "contract" has been arranged and a certain officer on the ship will soon be murdered. According to the caller, it is clear that the next-door neighbor wants to kill her husband for the insurance money, and she has already given the two "hit men" a down payment. The caller also provides rather detailed information on where and when the murder will take place. What do you do?

APPENDIX C
discussion of case studies

Do not paralyze our capacity for good by brooding over man's capacity for evil.

—Anonymous

Knowledge is not gained by words but by touch, sight, sound, victories, failures, sleeplessness, devotion, love—the human experiences and emotions of this earth and of oneself and other men, and perhaps too, a little faith, a little reverence for things you cannot see.

—Adlai Stevenson

The following paragraphs outline the action that was taken for each of the case studies highlighted in Appendix B. Some of the discussions are followed by brief analyses of the strengths and weaknesses of the leaders' decisions, as well as by lessons learned from the experience. All of these events occurred, but, in some cases, the circumstances have been modified slightly to avoid embarrassing those who were involved.

1. The Alcoholic Leader
The subordinate leader clearly had a problem, but he was so careful and so secretive about his alcoholism that it was hard to pinpoint conclusive evidence that he was drinking or drunk on the job. The leader called a private meeting with the subordinate leader's administrative assistant, and explained that her boss might be an alcoholic. Yet, since the leader was not absolutely certain about this, he asked the administrative assistant to track

her boss's behavior and whereabouts. She agreed to do this. For the next month or two, the assistant was able to keep a record, solely for the use of the leader, showing where her boss was and when and whether he showed signs of drinking during the day. The report clearly showed that the boss was drinking heavily at noontime. Sometimes, he would not return to work. If he did return, he would close his door and sit quietly in his office, instead of conducting business. After receiving this report, the leader met with his subordinate leader at mid-afternoon.

The leader told the subordinate that he was suspected of having a drinking problem. Furthermore, he requested that the subordinate go immediately to the hospital to take a blood test to measure his blood-alcohol level, and to get advice and counsel from the medical specialists there. The associate cooperated and the blood tests showed that although he had a very low level of alcohol in his blood, he did have liver damage and clearly was suffering from alcohol abuse. He was sent to an alcohol rehabilitation program at a hospital 100 miles away. After four weeks, he returned to his position.

The involvement of the administrative assistant was inappropriate; the leader, himself, should have tracked the activities of his subordinate. Also, it should not have taken many months to detect the presence of such a serious problem. However, sending the man to alcohol rehabilitation and allowing him to return to his position afterward were appropriate actions. Alcoholism is a disease, and it was important for the man's self-esteem and for the self-esteem of other people who might be suffering from drinking problems to realize that there is no punishment involved in the necessary treatment.

2. *Showdown with Your Banker*
The leader took the steps required to avoid exceeding the line of credit. By late February, the company was in great shape, and by April it had paid back the entire $16 million. Later that summer, the leader fired the banker. He set up an account with a bank that understands his business and keeps him informed well in advance about any concerns. The lesson here is that a company must have a close relationship with its bank or banks, and that

understanding, good communication, mutual respect, and trust should be the ground rules on all sides.

3. Integrity Problems Overseas

The leader worked closely with his top lawyer and the senior American in the headquarters, as well as with the local police. He was able to indict a number of the company officials. They received jail terms. The leader also called in the top foreign national and told him that it was time to accept early retirement, which the man did.

The major mistake that the leader made was not developing a coherent public relations approach. As a result, the leader and the company suffered from an extensive period of bad press that might have been avoided, at least in part. The lesson here may be that when a leader has to take very strong action, including sending his or her own employees to jail, a team of trusted associates needs to be assembled to ensure that the operational, legal, equal opportunity, public affairs, and integrity issues are addressed in a coordinated fashion.

4. An Associate Blows Up

This experience was very difficult because, despite all of the soothing language of the leader, the vice president took great offense. The leader was never able to convince his subordinate associate that the criticisms held some legitimate points. It turned out that the vice president was extremely sensitive in this regard; he was unable to weigh objectively constructive criticism. Further checking on the part of the leader revealed that the associate had problems in productively relating to others. The counselling session had uncovered a part of his personality of which the leader had not been aware. One lesson here is that a leader should not be afraid to criticize; criticism may uncover more than you expect. The leader should have removed the vice president from his position. He chose not to do so, since the vice president was less than a year away from retirement.

5. Drug Pushing by a Leader's Child

The plant manager was confronted directly, so that the leader could find out the background of the situation and what the manager would be willing to do about it. The plant manager was quite cavalier, maintaining that there was no big problem— that lots of kids were "doing drugs." The leader asked both the plant manager and his son to attend a drug rehabilitation program in order to ensure that they fully understood the consequences of drug involvement. If the plant manager had not been willing to attend drug rehabilitation with his son, he would have been fired. The lesson here is that it doesn't matter what position an associate holds; there will be opportunities for senior people, their children, and their spouses to get into trouble with drugs, theft, vandalism, and so forth. It is important for a leader to make it clear that major subordinate leaders have an even greater responsibility than others to set and maintain high standards for themselves and for members of their families.

6. Testifying Before Congress

The leader rightfully raised this issue during testimony, giving as much information to the committee as he had available on the test failure. He did this for a number of reasons. First, it would be wrong to withhold important information from a duly constituted congressional committee. Second, by withholding information, the leader would take the considerable risk of losing credibility and trust. At a later point, committee members and staffers might learn that there had been a failure and that the president possessed some information about it prior to his testimony that day. It is important to realize that the movement of a program through the Congress is a long and complex process that continues over a number of years. There are lots of opportunities for the Congress to withhold funds or cancel the program. A short-term victory often leads to a long-term defeat, if the quick victory is gained through manipulation of the facts or the withholding of information. Members of Congress and congressional staffers have long memories. Individuals who testify on Capitol Hill should realize that their most important assets are credibility and honesty.

7. Dealing with Child Molestation

The CEO fired the sports director for publicly embarrassing the newspaper and the publishing company. Many months later, the fired reporter approached the CEO and told him that he had spent all of his severance pay, that he could not find a job, and that he was destitute and desperate for work. After thoughtful consideration, the CEO called the editor of one of his periodicals in a distant location and asked the editor to give the man another chance. The situation was explained and it was requested that the editor not divulge the case to the other employees. Thus, the former sports director could get a fresh start.

The reporter settled into his new job and got married. He and his wife later had a baby. There were no more problems of sexual deviation. The lesson here is that in a very high visibility industry like public service or the media, very strong action is necessary. On the other hand, the CEO felt compassion for a talented man who, under the influence of alcohol, had made a terrible mistake. The period in which the reporter was completely out of work was a very sobering one in many ways. He has now found a new and happy life, thanks to the actions of a mature chief executive officer who was willing to give someone a second chance.

8. Moonlighting by a Key Associate

The CEO called in the division chief and explained that there seemed to be a clear conflict of interest. He had to ask the division chief to give up this independent business and spend his full time on company matters. The employee said that he could not accept that plan, but he was willing to discuss other available options. After some discussion during which the employee stuck with his position of keeping his independent company going, the CEO said, "I think you have just resigned and I think I have just accepted your resignation." The lesson here is clear. When hiring new employees, and especially ones who will be in leadership positions, it is important to make the work rules very specific. It is best to put these rules in writing, so there can be no misunderstanding on either side. The CEO, by agreeing to "some teaching on the side," made a mistake. Since the division chief was hired for a brand-new enterprise, it would have been better to ask him to put all of his efforts into his work and request that he do outside things only after he won some contracts. The employee, by using so much of the company's time and resources to support his independent business, made a serious mistake that cost him his job. The whole enterprise cost the company about a million dollars, with no positive results. The CEO said it was his worst mistake in ten years of running the company.

9. Empowerment Problems Overseas

This leader found that he had a major task. He had to explain the philosophies of matrix management to all of his employees through the processes of meetings, written memos, training sessions, etc. He had to describe the changes in company approach to all of his major customers, many of whom not only didn't understand it, but also were uncomfortable with it. The education process went on for years, and only over an extended time did understanding and support evolve. The lesson here is that the cultural environment of an overseas subsidiary does not change easily. Top executives must be careful not to design a management model that may work well in Chicago or Los Angeles, but may function poorly in New Delhi or Rio.

10. Trouble with Your Sports Fans

The university president wrote an article about decorum and conduct at football games, and published it in the school newspaper. Then, at a sporting event, he sat down among the rowdy students and began to talk to them in a friendly way. He let them know that he was interested in their having a good time, and that he would be with them for the rest of the game. It soon became clear that the students were willing to be more careful about what they said and what they did. The fact that some of them had read the president's article helped. The president later wrote additional articles on this subject. Although the problem did not completely go away, it did diminish during the rest of the season. The lesson learned here is that whenever you have a large number of people congregating at a sporting event, there is always the possibility of drinking before the game, violation of the no-alcohol rule in the stadium, and harassment of the other team, its cheerleaders, or its fans. The president, or a senior university official who is well-known in the university community, should attend major sporting events and intervene diplomatically but firmly in any situation that appears to be getting out of hand. This technique also is useful in identifying troublemakers, so that they can be disciplined.

11. Dealing with Suicide

The school principal immediately activated the school district's crisis response team and her own crisis response team. She got on the public address system and explained what she knew about the situation. The principal also gave the students some free time to gather together and talk about their thoughts on the tragedy. She worked very closely with the parents on the funeral and memorial events. In fact, the principal volunteered to participate in the funeral and to give the eulogy. She suggested that the school set up a memorial and a scholarship in the student's honor. A fund drive would contribute to these new endeavors.

The principal immediately tended to the needs of all who were involved. She responded with attention, concern, information, and new ideas. At the time of a totally unexpected tragedy, people expect a great deal from the person in charge. The leader must be willing to break the routine, drop the scheduled activities, and act quickly, decisively, and compassionately.

12. Hiring the Overly Ambitious

Clearly, the individual about whom the letters were being written was spending a great deal of his time working on a possible future assignment. He was very ambitious and very "careerist," asking many officials to go to bat for him. It was evident that he was not spending much of his time concentrating on his present job. The planning director sent letters to the officials, thanking them for their interest. All were informed that the individual had not been selected to work in the department. Sometimes, the individuals who are so interested in getting just the right assignment actually end up "shooting themselves in the foot." By coming across as being hyperambitious and unwilling to trust the personnel system to do its job well, this person struck out. Hyperambition hurts many talented people. Leaders occasionally should caution their subordinates collectively and, when appropriate, individually about not getting caught in the trap of careerism.

13. Keeping Secrets
You are in a very delicate area here. It is important to be forthright with the media while, at the same time, guarding very sensitive and highly classified information. The assistant secretary answered it in the following way: "This is an area of great concern. We are pursuing a number of technological solutions in hopes of developing a weapons system that will fill this gap." If, in such a situation, the reporter continues to press for information, the best approach is probably to follow up by saying, "These technologies are of such a sensitive nature that it would be inappropriate for me to comment on the specifics."

14. Intimidation by a Union Boss
The mayor picked up the phone in his office and handed it to the head of the fireman's union. He told him to go ahead and call the fire stations as he had threatened to do, but to be sure to tell everyone that those who participated in this illegal action would be fired permanently. He gave the union boss another choice—to sit down and discuss this issue calmly and rationally. After expressing his views in rather colorful language, the union boss sat down with the mayor. In turn, the mayor talked to the fire commission. The suspension was withheld and the crisis was averted. A new and more professional examination was designed, and a more foolproof examination system was created. The professionalism of the entire fire department was enhanced. This example shows that, as a leader, it is important not to allow yourself to be intimidated. When someone tries to bully you, be ready with a strong countervailing approach.

15. Dealing with a Death Threat
The ship's commander called in a small group of his staff, as well as the FBI, to do a preliminary investigation of this situation and to gather advice. When it became clear that the facts

substantiated the telephone caller's information, the commander called in the officer and quietly laid out the situation to him. Although the officer initially did not believe the commander, he changed his mind when all the facts were presented. The FBI set a trap and the officer went to the spot where the murder was to take place. The two "hit men" were apprehended and, along with the officer's wife, were indicted for and convicted of attempted murder. All three were sent to jail.

APPENDIX D
leadership education programs

*To every man there comes in his lifetime that special moment
when he is figuratively tapped on the shoulder and offered that
chance to do a very special thing, unique to him and his talents.
What a tragedy if that moment finds him unprepared or
unqualified for that work.*

—Winston Churchill

I am a great believer in formal education for leaders and future
leaders, and am particularly taken by programs that accomplish
a great deal in a fairly short time. In the following pages, I recommend a few of the very best programs that are available in
the United States. Each of these programs provides opportunities for growth, introspection, and insight. They also allow
attendees to get to know one another. The learning that occurs
between and among the students is one of the major benefits of
these workshops. Anyone who is a leader, or is expecting to
move into a leadership position within the next few years, who
has not already attended one of these programs should try hard
to do so. It will be an invaluable experience.

The *Blue Ridge Conference on Leadership* is a three-day conference
held in the lovely Blue Ridge mountains near Ashville, North
Carolina. Each July, it attracts about 900 leaders and potential
leaders. There are four aspects of this program that are especially attractive. First, the speeches and workshops are dynamic
and uplifting. Second, the cost of the conference is quite modest.
Third, the setting is peaceful and relaxed. And finally, there are

lots of opportunities for interaction among the participants. This program is designed to help working people who already have some leadership responsibilities, but aspire to move up in their companies. It attracts managers from small- and medium-sized companies throughout the South. Blue Ridge Conference on Leadership, 1430 W Peachtree Street NW, Suite 607, Atlanta, GA 30309–2937; (404) 881–1110.

The *Center for Creative Leadership* at Greensboro, North Carolina, has a well-deserved reputation for excellence. Started in the early 1970s with a generous and long-term commitment from the Smith Richardson Foundation, the CCL has grown to a staff of about 200, about one-fourth of whom are involved in research. The Center is particularly strong in the behavioral sciences; the psychological testing and evaluation program is one of the very best in the world. The CCL has a variety of programs that last from four to six days, several of which focus on creativity and innovation in organizations. Many are held at the modern and marvelously equipped facility at Greensboro, while others are held at various locations throughout the country and overseas. Center for Creative Leadership, PO Box 26301, Greensboro, NC 27438–6301; (910) 282–3284.

The *Gallup Leadership Institute* runs a five-day program at which participants learn about their own leadership talents and how they can increase levels of performance for themselves and their associates. Through the use of a structured interview, a written profile, and an individual consultation, participants discover more about their leadership strengths and how to leverage them most effectively. They develop a leadership plan to meet the specific challenges that they face. A remeasurement component allows participants to assess the impact of their leadership talents in the workplace over time. Gallup Leadership Institute, 301 South 68th Street Place, Lincoln, NE 68510; 1–800–288–8592.

Along with the service academies, the *Jepson School of Leadership Studies* ranks as one of the best undergraduate programs in leadership in the United States. The teaching methods at the Jepson

School rely on mentoring, role-playing, hands-on community service projects, internships, and other application-oriented methods. This program aims to combine academic knowledge and experiential learning, to set the path for life-long, self-directed education. The teaching and learning environment resembles a working community, with the instructor as a partner. Upon graduation, the student receives an undergraduate degree in leadership. Jepson School of Leadership Studies, University of Richmond, Richmond, VA 23173; (804) 287–6062.

The *Kellogg National Leadership Program* was established in the late 1970s and provides a three-year, part-time scholarship program for people in this country who have a high potential for top leadership. Every other year, between forty and fifty men and women are selected (out of about 1,000 applicants). Varying in age from the late twenties to the mid-forties, these mature participants already have demonstrated a desire to lead people. They are selected by a team of distinguished individuals who not only review each application carefully, but also interview approximately 100 of the most qualified candidates. Each new group assembles for a week of orientation and education on leadership. In recent years, it has been my pleasure to be one of the kickoff speakers. Each fellow must choose a learning plan and study a leadership issue in an area completely outside his or her chosen profession. Over the course of the next three years, the group gets together about every six months, for a one- or two-week session (including a two-week session in an overseas nation). The fellows are given sufficient funds to buy a personal computer and to do research on the learning plan. The Foundation also pays for the modem and the telephone costs that allow access to the internet through their personal computers. Kellogg National Leadership Program, 1 East Michigan Avenue, Battle Creek, MI 49017–3398; (616) 968–1611.

Community Leadership Programs. Numerous cities throughout the United States have excellent leadership programs. These programs serve many purposes. First, they teach leadership to people in management positions throughout the community. They also are excellent vehicles for getting bright and hard-working people together, so that they will get to know each other well. Third, most of these programs have an alumni program, allowing people from the various groups to interact. Most of these programs run for a year. Leadership fellows usually meet once a month and take a close look at one aspect of the community— for example, the fire department, the police department, the mayor's office, a major local hospital, one or more of the local businesses.

One of the very best of these programs is *Leadership Erie.* A remarkable organizer and teacher, Dr. David Kozak, a professor at Gannon University, has established a program of great substance and diversity. He brings in some of the most outstanding speakers in the country to supplement the talents of the local leaders and teachers. Each participant is given a leadership tool kit, an easy-to-use guide to leadership at the grass roots level. Kozak is most willing to share with others throughout the nation what he has learned from building and raising money for this program. Leadership Erie, PO Box 842, Erie, PA 16512; (814) 871–7231.

Military Programs. The military has some excellent programs at the various service academies and war colleges, as well as at the mid-level staff colleges. In addition, each of the services has a leadership center: the Navy at Norfolk, Virginia; the Army at Fort Leavenworth, Kansas; the Air Force at Montgomery, Alabama; and the Marine Corps at Quantico, Virginia. The services also do research on leadership. For example, the Army Research Institute in Alexandria, Virginia has an active leadership research program at both the small-unit level and the executive level. Although the military programs generally are closed to people outside the federal government, many civilian employees of the federal government have opportunities to attend the war and staff colleges. In addition, the military sponsors research on leadership with many universities and research centers.

University Programs. There are a number of first-rate leadership development programs run by universities around the country.

These programs normally run for four or five weeks. Although they are quite expensive and demand a great deal of hard work, they are certainly worthwhile. Some of the very best include: Executive Leadership Program, School of Business Administration of the University of Southern California, Los Angeles, CA 90089, (213) 740–8990; Columbia Senior Executive Program, Columbia Business School, Columbia University, 2880 Broadway, 480 Armstrong Hall, New York, NY 10025, (212) 854–6015; Leading and Managing Change, Graduate School of Business, Stanford University, Stanford, CA 94305, (415) 723–7552; Program for Strategic Leadership, Smeal College of Business Administration, 310 Business Administration Building, University Park, PA 16802, (814) 865–3435.

These programs are but a few of the many leadership education and executive development programs that are available. Many are specifically designed to attract leaders from diverse backgrounds. The purpose is not only to allow much of the learning to take place among the students, but also to help leaders within a city, a region, or a community to know and understand one another better. Even those leaders who feel they do not need these programs should participate upon occasion—as much for the contacts they make and the contributions they can provide to others as for what they can learn themselves. If successful leaders are willing to help other leaders and potential leaders who do not have the same skills, experience, and wisdom, the nation will be served well.

APPENDIX E
suggested reading list

How many a man has dated a new era in his life from the reading of a book.

—*Henry David Thoreau*

You are the same today that you are going to be five years from now except for two things: the people with whom you associate, and the books you read.

—*Charles Jones*

The literature on leadership is rich and diverse. However, individuals often have difficulty finding the books that are the most relevant to their own challenges and opportunities. Having read more than 500 books on leadership, I have chosen those books which provide the most useful insights and practical advice.

Bennis, Warren, and Burt Nanus. *Leaders: The Strategy of Taking Charge.* New York: Harper and Row.

Bennis offers quite persuasive insights on the following areas of leadership: infusing organizations with energy; creating a culture of pride; teachership; the empowerment of subordinate leaders; and avoiding activities that waste people's time.

Blanchard, Kenneth, and Spencer Johnson. *The One-Minute Manager.* New York: William Morrow and Company.

This short book is a quick-read that contains useful insights into the value of delegating.

Bramson, Robert. *Coping with Difficult People.* New York: Dell
    Publishing.
This book should be kept at the elbow of every leader. Dr. Bramson
doesn't tell you how to fix difficult people, he tells you something
more useful and realistic—how to cope with difficult bosses, peers,
and subordinates.

Burns, James McGregor. *Leadership.* New York: Harper and Row.
This Pulitzer Prize and National Book Award-winning book concen-
trates on political leadership. Burns' discussion of transactional and
transforming leadership is tremendously insightful. For those readers
who don't have time to read the entire work, I recommend the por-
tions that focus on transformation.

Carter, Stephen L. *Integrity.* New York: Basic Books.
A brilliant analysis of the most important factor in leadership—
integrity.

Collins, James C., and Jerry I. Porras. *Built to Last: Successful Habits of
    Visionary Companies.* New York: HarperCollins Publishers.
This work explains how and why General Electric, Disney, MMM,
Sony, and others have remained so successful for so long.

Depree, Max. *Leadership Is an Art.* New York: Dell Publishing.
The best short book on leadership written by someone who has run a
large corporation.

Deep, Sam, and Lyle Sussman. *Smart Moves for People in Charge.*
    Reading, MA: Addison-Wesley Publishing.
If you like checklists, this book is for you; 130 checklists are provided
to help people be better leaders. It also includes lots of fine quotes and
"one liners."

Dougherty, Devon. *Crisis Communications: What Every Executive Needs
    to Know.* New York: Walker and Company.
To be read *before* Sam Donaldson is in your face.

Drucker, Peter. *The New Realities.* New York: Harper and Row.
Any of Drucker's writing on leadership is well-worth reading.

Grove, Andy. *Only the Paranoid Survive.* New York: Doubleday Publishing.

The extraordinary story of Intel, a remarkable American company, by the man most responsible for its success.

Hart, Michael H. *The 100: A Ranking of the Most Influential Persons in History.* Secaucus, NJ: Citadel Press.

A thought-provoking analysis of history's most influential people, many of whom were also great leaders.

Hegelsen, Sally. *The Female Advantage.* New York: Doubleday Publishing.

Although the first sixty pages of this book are a little slow-going, the rest is a brilliant analysis of how women use their skills to be outstanding leaders.

Matusak, Larraine. *Finding Your Voice: Learning to Lead...Anywhere You Want to Make a Difference.* San Francisco: Jossey-Bass Publishing.

This is a book for the grass roots leader. Dr. Matusak ran the marvelous Kellogg National Leadership Program for many years.

Pogue, Forrest. *George C. Marshall.* 4 vols. New York: Viking Press.

This four-volume series is the best biography on this extraordinary American military leader. The second volume is the best of the collection.

Powell, Colin. *An American Journey.* New York: Random House.

This is a modern Horatio Alger story written by the best American public servant since George Marshall. Many leadership insights can be gained from this uplifting work.

Shaara, Michael. *The Killer Angels.* New York: David McKay Co.

This is probably the best historical novel on leadership available in print today. The novel is approximately 98 percent accurate. Only the specific words uttered by Lee, Longstreet, and others are not and cannot be historically precise.

Stross, Randall. *The Microsoft Way.* Reading, MA: Addison-Wesley Publishing.

The best book on the leadership paradigm that Bill Gates and Steve Ballmer have established at Microsoft.

von Clausewitz, Karl. *On War,* translated by Michael Howard and
  Peter Paret. Princeton, NJ: Princeton University Press.

This classic on strategy has a particularly perceptive chapter on military genius (pages 100–112). This chapter should be mandatory reading for all students of leadership.

I would like to recognize my favorite authors, whose books
on leaders and leadership are especially powerful: Jim Stockdale;
Forrest Pogue; Warren Bennis; Peter Drucker; Max Depree;
Stephen Ambrose; Steve Covey; Edmund Morris; Michael
Howard; Martin Blumenson; and William Manchester.

In addition to reading good books, you can gain insights on
a whole range of issues relating to leadership by regularly reading three magazines: *Business Week; The Economist;* and *The
Futurist.* There also are outstanding audiotape series produced
by Nightingale Conant (call 1–800–323–5552). I recommend the
following: *How Leaders Lead* by Ken Blanchard and Brian Tracy;
The Seven Habits of Highly Effective People by Steve Covey; and
Coping with Difficult People by Robert Bramson.

ABOUT THE AUTHOR

Perry M. Smith is an internationally known speaker, TV commentator, best-selling author, and the president of Visionary Leadership of Augusta, Georgia. He has conducted seminars on leadership, strategic planning, and ethics for hundreds of organizations, including Harvard's Kennedy School; George Washington University; Forging Industry Association; Century 21; UPS; Texas Instruments; Springs Industries; Caterpillar; Ford; Fifth Third Bank; The Chautauqua Institution; West Virginia Hospital Association; Andersen Consulting; WK Kellogg Foundation; Tiffany & Company; Canon; Microsoft; Time Warner; Lockheed Martin; the governors of two states; and the mayor of Detroit. Smith also gives keynote speeches at conferences and conventions. In addition, he has served CNN as its military analyst.

A retired major general, Smith served in the U.S. Air Force for thirty years. During his military career, he held a number of leadership positions, including command of the F-15 wing in Germany. During that assignment, he provided leadership to 4,000 personnel. Later, Smith served as the top Air Force planner. He also was the Commandant of the National War College, where he taught courses on leadership of large and complex organizations and on strategic planning.

General Smith is a graduate of the U.S. Military Academy at West Point, and earned his Ph.D. in International Relations from Columbia University. His dissertation (on planning) earned the Helen Dwight Reid Award from the American Political Science Association. He has written five books, including *Assignment Pentagon* (Brassey's U.S.) and *How CNN Fought the War* (Birch Lane Press).

The first two editions of *Rules & Tools for Leaders*, then titled

Taking Charge, sold more than 200,000 copies. The text is used in many leadership and executive development programs in corporations, non-profit organizations, government agencies, and military professional schools. *Taking Charge* has been translated into Spanish, Chinese, Indonesian, and Turkish.

Smith's next book will be a biography of his father-in-law, Lieutenant Colonel Jimmie Dyess, USMCR. Dyess is the only person to have earned America's two highest awards for heroism: The Carnegie Medal and the Medal of Honor. Dyess was killed in combat on the Marshall Islands on February 2, 1944.

Perry Smith lives with his wife in Augusta, Georgia. His wife, formerly Connor Cleckley Dyess, is a lyric soprano who has sung for Presidents Ford and Carter, and was the featured soloist at Jimmie Doolittle's 90th birthday. The Smiths have two children, McCoy and Serena, and two granddaughters, Dyess and Porter.

INDEX